Out of the Clear

I0866700

Erin Manning

<.:.MinOr.:.>
.cOmpOsitiOns.

Out of the Clear
Erin Manning

ISBN 978-1-57027-405-3

Cover design by Haduhi Szukis
Page 21: "The West Wind," Tom Thomson (1917)
Interior design by Casandra Johns (www.houseofhands.net)
Copyediting by Emma Flavian

Released by Minor Compositions 2023
Colchester / New York / Port Watson

Minor Compositions is a series of interventions & provocations drawing from autonomous politics, avant-garde aesthetics, and the revolutions of everyday life.

Minor Compositions is an imprint of Autonomedia
www.minorcompositions.info | minorcompositions@gmail.com

Distributed by Autonomedia
PO Box 568 Williamsburgh Station
Brooklyn, NY 11211

www.autonomedia.org
info@autonomedia.org

Table of Contents

with Brian, always.

Foreword

A year ago, we were mapling for the first time, completely unexpectedly. We had purchased the 3Ecologies land a month before and were expecting the original owners to do the sugaring off the first year while we learned alongside. As with almost everything around the purchase of the land, nothing turned out the way we expected. I did get a lesson from them, but it was just an hour or two, and then we were on our own.

We had been working toward the 3E project for a dozen years by then. In the transversality of the social, the conceptual and the environmental, the orientation of 3E was always to amplify those modes of encounter that facilitate living and learning. We dreamed of a site for experimentation that could facilitate radical pedagogies and foster the practice of alter-economic living. Originally, we thought we would purchase a triplex in Montreal and that it would become the alter-economic/alter-pedagogical site for the proposition. The land came to us unexpectedly at a time when the prices in Montreal were moving increasingly out of reach and we were less and less sure our alter-economic experiment, the 3E Process Seed Bank, would ever prove financially viable. Then the pandemic hit and SenseLab bore the familiar brunt of a reduction of the liveliness of minor sociality to Zoom squares. We tried hard to imagine other ways – parking lot bookrooms, kite-making workshops – but over the almost two years of lockdowns, it became harder and harder to craft sociality. For the almost twenty years of SenseLab, lurking had been a life-giving practice – to attend sideways was vital to all our activities. This modality of practicing-alongside became less and less feasible given the conditions not only of the COVID restrictions themselves, but of a more systemic dampening of the liveliness of collective experience as the months became a year, and one year became two. As time passed, a kind of inertia set in, I think, that made it more and more difficult to find our way back to the techniques we had honed so carefully. New techniques needed to be crafted, this at a time when collective invention was at its most threatened.

The land purchase happened extremely quickly. Brian Massumi and I went to see an off-grid solar house three hours north of Montreal, heard there was more land, and that there was a second house, saw the maple shack and the cabin next to it and the old growth maple forest, and we were in! A big debt was taken on, and we scrambled to make the mid-pandemic shift work. A lot had to be managed at once, least of which was that we didn't own a car and so had no easy way to get there! A lovely student and collaborator came through, offering us his car. This generosity – of time, of techniques – has continued to amaze us, as we find our uncertain footing.

This book arrives at that moment where we are waiting for the sap to run for the second time. Exactly a year has passed, but the temperature is much colder and we've had more snow, so according to local lore, the trees will take their time because their feet are cold.

Things feel different. After a year of scrambling to understand how to keep the houses running given the challenges of solar energy in the north, especially in the early months of winter when the sun is low, a year spent troubleshooting generators that refused to start, water pumps that exploded (more than once!), dealing with rodent and insect infestations; a year spent learning how to regenerate the soil and grow fruit trees, how to renature the creek and prepare for a future micro-hydro installation; a year spent agonizing over cutting trees and hauling wood and building woodsheds and stacking wood from one place to another, and then to another; a year spent splitting wood and making kindling and starting fires and making beds and more beds for rental guests in the aim of making the project economically viable; a year spent cleaning and renovating the small cabin next to the sugar shack, so many collaborators facilitating, each step not yet enough but so much already, we are here, ready to boil the sap again.

This time around another thousand things will go wrong, no doubt. Just this morning when connecting the hose to the large vat that gathers the sap, we noticed it was eaten right through! This after fixing it the day before yesterday after the bulldozer that ploughed the snow ripped it apart along with the electrical cord linking the two off-grid buildings. Tomorrow we will repair it again. And after that something else will go wrong. The difference is, we are more practiced about how to go about learning how to fix things, and we know more people who are there when we need to figure out where to begin.

When the boiling of the sap begins, an alchemy sets in. The shack, a beautifully dilapidated space, takes on a strange quality, at once a site of slow watchfulness, our collective eye on the thermometer, awaiting the tantalizing 219 degrees, and a site of frenetic energy, as we work breathlessly to keep the fire hot, keeping the foam low on the maple vats. The sap is boiled down in a ratio of forty to one, and this is a long process, the first boil easily lasting twelve hours. Last year there were days when we boiled all day without reaching the necessary 67 Brix before running out of sap. We would go to bed defeated, hoping to get more sap the next day. Eternal Return, one of our later batches, took two days! Of course no seasoned syruper will tell such tales. They are better at building fires than we are, and most of them have technological help: evaporators and osmosis machines. We do it the old way, with lots of wood, lots of time, and lots of collaborators.

This book wrote itself in those interstices when the questions became so urgent that I needed to address them directly. That's always been my way: to begin in practice and, when lost, to reorient through writing. The orientations remain troubled: how to reconcile the larger ecological footprint (generators, cars, propane appliances) with the project (3ecological living)? How to tweak the visual modalities for ecological housing to facilitate ProTactile collaboration? So much of what is in place to foster ecological living requires a certain kind of ableism – the ability to make and sustain wood fires, the management of the batteries through visual screens, the necessity to keep pilot lights lit. How to keep the process neurodiverse, to avoid overcoding it with neurotypical expectations? There is also all the snow shoveling, the wood hauling, the chainsaw handling. What kinds of processes could be put in place to run the houses and make the project viable such that it didn't rely on a single set of physical skills? And, how to manage the collective necessities without falling into the model of a community? How to retain the attunement toward the minor such that the coming-together can also thrive in a sidling posture? How to be in the midst without being in common? How to foster modes of living alongside that open the way for undercommon conviviality? And how to teach each other not to rely on the kind of returns investments in property promise, moving instead to propositions attuned toward a more-than human commitment to the surrounds on land that will never again be privately owned, bought or sold? What is it to live without the promise of inheritance?

After several years working on a cryptoeconomic proposition for alter-economic futures we know something about complicity, and about strategic duplicity. This is what we take into this project, and what this book explores.

The 3E land purchase is not a back to the land project. It's an opening toward what else the transversality of the three ecologies – the social, the conceptual and the environmental – can propose, in overlap.

Concepts have always felt like friends. The impersonal looms large, as does minor sociality, and speculative pragmatism. In an echo of *For a Pragmatics of the Useless* (2020), this is a book that propels the logic of the approximation of proximity of black life and neurodiversity toward the living-forth on a tract of land that has pushed us beyond our limits and more often than not kept us from our writing. What has moved into book form here pushed its way onto the page out of necessity, with Nietzschean force. It largely emerged as scenes, the force of encounter leading the way. *Was that life? Well then, once more!*

Out of the Clear

Prelude

"When there is nothing to govern, nothing to secure, there is blackness." (Harney and Moten 2021, 84)

Scene 1

Barkskins, a novel by Annie Proulx, is a literary account of the violence of clearing that was endemic to settler colonialism in Canada and the Northern US at the time of early colonization by the French, and later the English. Starting with the early arrival in the 1600s and continuing to the multi-generational raping of the land by the steady influx of colonizers, the book relentlessly marks the passage from plenitude to desecration, the forests denuded at the cost of upheaval and death of the people who had never sought to clear them. This story is ultimately not about the trees, of course, but about the violence of cultural clearing and the genocide it leaves behind. And yet it is also about the trees, about those enormous pines, the forests unimaginable, the pristine "before" when lands were rich and people lived out of the clear.

As these accounts do, the story begins with a French man, Trépigny, and though First Nations characters make their way into the story and even become main characters, the reader never forgets that it is the colonizer who enters first, and who makes the first cut.

The scene is as we expect it: black flies, mud, rain, "dark vast forest, inimical wilderness" (Proulx 2016, 3). "How big is the forest?" one of the early colonizers asks. "It is the forest of the world. It is infinite. It twists around as a snake swallows its own tail and has no end and no beginning. No one has seen its farthest dimension" (4). The first tree – made into a great old single board pine table – serves as a motif for all that has been violently stolen, for all that has been falsely claimed into ownership, for all that has been condoned in the cementing of the notion that nature is owed and owned. The table, which will eventually be bequeathed to the half-breed daughter by the white colonizer father, will be fought over, claimed by his sons. They will argue that the Indian cannot see its value, that she has no use for it, and that it is rightfully theirs. She will appease them, agreeing that she does not see its value. “She rapped her knuckles on the pine. She said she did not know why Outger was so passionate about it. He asked after it in every letter and would undoubtedly be angry when she told him it was gone” (254).

She will not lay claim to it, will refuse to see the value it has in the white man’s eyes, but she will also refuse to give it back. Because the table, she understands, represents the experiment that she has become. “I can see now [...] that all his pedagogy was an experiment. The books and instruction had been his attempt to make her into something like a learned whiteman, like himself” (292). Unclaimed, the table will have done its work, teaching her with all the demoralizing splendor that comes with colonization that she can neither inhabit the world of the white man nor, ultimately, become Indian enough, no matter how much she tries. “‘But,’ she said sadly, ‘I could not become an Indian.’ ‘Of course not,’ said Dr. Mukhtar. ‘There is a whole world of signs, symbols and spirits which all must be absorbed from birth. You could not hope to grasp the meanings except by living the entire life'" (292). The table stays as the scar of a life stolen. Eventually, it will fall into oblivion, like the rest of the "largest white pines that ever grew in the world" (322) but the memory of its infinitude, of all the potential violated, will continue to haunt the clearing.

Scene 2

We already know how the story ends. On May 29th 2021, the headline reads: "Canada mourns as remains of 215 children found at indigenous school."[1] It wasn't an Indigenous school, of course. It was a residential school, a Canadian school, in the clearing. The picture says it all: sparse trees growing in the background, empty yard, an architecture completely at odds with the environment, cleared of life, of all that immanently interconnects. The violence of logistics is inscribed in the ghost trees of its whitened surround.

How we organize bodies, we who sidle whiteness, how we excise (from clear sight) the ravages of an earth desecrated, of a people brutally

1 "Canada mourns as remains of 215 children found at indigenous school," *BBC* online, May 29, 2021, https://www.bbc.com/news/world-us-canada-57291530.

murdered – these are the workings of logistics. Logistics mediate existence by keeping it at arm's length, soothing us into believing that we are not responsible. The deaths are newsworthy, and we're sorry, but we must move on. It's not really about us and in any case, there's nothing we can do about it. Let's get a mediator and sort this out!

At arms length, we see these workings – the cleared forest, the dying planet, the dead children – as somehow disconnected. We do not acknowledge the felling of the trees as the wanton destruction of all that transversally connects. And yet logistics, in its power of mediation, is all about the forests. It's all about the cotton planted in their wake.

The ghostly outline of Proulx's pine table haunts the residential school, its absence equal to the absence of education. Because what the residential school really does is unteach. Taking the place of pedagogy, what is practiced there is theft. Theft of thought, of imagination. This theft is a rape. A physical rape, a sexual aggression, but also a conceptual rape, a clearing – "to snatch, to grab, to carry off by force" – of all that lives in the abyss of what has been left behind.[2] Rape, relation severed, cuts the fragile interwoven threads of existence, wresting life from life-living, from the more-than that gives it its spirited and spiritual contour. If body is land, if bodying is only ever worlding, what residential school does, in this most recent form of clearing, is sever this imbrication, leaving the body lifeless.

All that remains is the clearing. And a mess. But this can be handled. This is how mediation does its work, in the name of and as logistics. From here on in, things will be managed. Managers will be appointed to organize, to administer, the now-reduced environment. This science of loss – "which is to say the science of whiteness, or logistics" (Harney and Moten 2021, 14) – is predicated on the end of sharing, on the destruction of the excessive share, the annihilation of that which exceeds the one-two form whose dramaturgy relies of the intervention of

2 *Oxford English Dictionary*, 2nd edition (1989), s.v. "rape."

the mediator. The mediator will take the form of the "yellow eyebrows" in Proulx's account, but it also need not take a simple human form. Repetition of the same is the form it takes in a dramaturgy of extinction.

Scene 3

Clearing produces property. Property produces dispossession. "All property is loss because all property is the loss of sharing" (Harney and Moten 2021, 14). The accursed share of all that exceeds interpersonality, mediation, whiteness, logistics, all that cannot be accounted for, sickens the field. And sometimes rejuvenates it. The force of the transindividual, of all that exceeds and precedes the individual, does rewild. But its vitality is weakened, and as perception is honed to single out the individual over the field, the human increasingly becomes the focal point, becoming synonymous with life. This is how the logistics of genocide – the genocide of relation – does its work.

The genocide of relation can never be traced back, quite. Relation cannot be propertied. What is lost cannot be parsed. The yellow eyebrows have a role to play, of course, and we could call on the archbishop for that missing apology, but the truth is, it was never just one. He was never just the one. He is a logistical pattern, a commitment to the dramaturgy of (white) man as self-centered orchestrator of existence cleared.

Scene 4

Logistics: the slave ship, but also the body-as-individual. "The first odious vessel produced by and for logistics is not the slave ship, but the body – flesh conceptualized – which bears the individual-in-subjection" (Harney and Moten 2021, 14).

In the clearing, man is revealed as the loss of relation. Humanism is born here, in the empty space of the stolen land, in the vast expanse of the 1+1, the infinite regress of nothing-in-between.

How to fill the emptiness? How to create an account for all that is lost and yet claimed?

Mediation offers to fill the shape of the between. Mediation as the figure of what comes between, of what fills that "empty" space. The adjuster, the divorce lawyer, the priest, the government agent.

A quick intervention to make sense of all that has become unclear, to fill in the lines, to provide context.

And perhaps this does make things clearer, perhaps we understand each other a bit better now that we've mediated all we couldn't make sense of in the vast emptiness of our difference. But the problem is: mediation never goes away. It sits there, inert but active, facilitating the ongoing impoverishment of relation by adhering to all that takes the shape of the 1 + 1 of body-as-individual, of interpersonality. Because in advance of the gesture of inserting the mediating influence, he is already there. Long before the divorce, he hovers, betweener, judging, parsing, condoning, condemning. His take doesn't really matter. What matters is that he remains in the offing, holding things apart.

Mediation is the father of the control society. It is the way surveillance takes on a personality from the outside in. Whether formally or informally, mediation sets the tone for an interpersonality that, by definition, can only be lived at a distance. Playing at impartiality, mediation haunts the surround, reducing it to what is already known, what is already valued, what is already within the scope of the expressible. 2 + 1, always less than 3, mediation is passive aggressor, poised for judgment, always in the know (while it listens carefully). Because its role is to keep existence in its track, on its logistical path. It doesn't really matter who is right. It matters that it needs mediation.

Mediation knows best, trampling on any detail of middling, sewing interactivity into a twoness without excess. Hardening the between of interpersonality into the amplification of the self-same, mediation lodges at the interstice, cutting it into a hyphen, setting up its colony on the bridge. Settler, it speaks from a place it has never had to truly encounter because its role is only to order things apart.

Moten and Harney might speak of mediation with the same disdain as they do of logistics, which they call the "science of whiteness" (2021, 14). Mediation is the logistic category par excellence of whiteness. It has no content, is not in itself an agent of transformation, does nothing but cannibalize the life it parses. Its intervention happens in the beat of enter and retreat, leaving the uneasy twoness of existence to sort itself out. In the name of property and propriety, mediation solves all uncertainties of zoning. That it never actually leaves is its dirty secret.

But the logistics of mediation can only fail. The interface is shaky – we know this both from the endemic code 404, page not found, and from the impossibility of truly domesticating our surrounds. Ultimately, the squirrels, the black flies, the birds, the worms, the fungi, the weeds, the viruses, the hackers cannot be kept in their place. The disarray is handled, of course, with more mediation, with more logistics.

The interface claims a distance, a secure between-two that repeats the refrain of nature colonized, of culture denatured. It promises a security of inhabitation, a zone that can be controlled, a slip through which we can safely enter, we who claim the place. Here, in the logistics of passage that beats at the cadence of the one-two, me-you, the outcome is always the same. Police to subjugate. Code to organize. Clear to colonize.

> Logistics aims to straighten us out, untangle us, and open us to its usufruct, its improving use; such access to us, in its turn, improves the flow line, the straight line. And what logistics takes to be the shortest distance between us requires emplotting us as bodies in space where interiority can be imposed even as the capacity for interiority can be denied, in the constant measure and regulation of flesh and earth. (Harney and Moten 2021, 18)

Scene 5

Deleuze and Guattari speak of man as the white wall of the black hole of existence (1987, 167). Think landscape painting, especially the kind that excises that very life that breathed it into existence. If you're not familiar, search for "Canadian art." And if you don't know the history of the mansplaining of the Canadian landscape, search for the Group of Seven, the early twentieth-century Canadian landscape painters, and notice not only the ubiquity of the vast open, uninhabited space, notice the clearing. Very little has changed over the last hundred years. We still see Canada through the clear, in the emptiness of nature cultured.

The denuded land, the empty north, is how we art ourselves still today, we who property the land. The Group of Seven, those painters of the land pristine, of the great white north, the painters of the land of the (single) pine and of the distant ridges, they are still with us, still managing the imagination, orchestrating the field, playing the dramaturgy of extinction. Logistics are also aesthetic (if not artful).

The white man is a specter. That is to say, the white man is without content, without shape. He is the shift in form that allows all takings-place

to be propertied inhabitations, which is to say, sites already claimed. This is whiteness: the pretense that the lines that demarcate the boundary between me and you protect you, protect me, from the wilderness of all that cannot be contained (and must be kept at bay). The truth is, the wilderness was cleared, but never quite colonized. And that is why whiteness is alive and well. To police a job half-done.

Scene 6

Mediation makes many promises. It promises clarity: think, drop-down menu. It promises fairness: think, divorce court. It promises health: think, therapy. The gesture is cast as innocuous. A simple third, a neutral agent. A little bit of reason. A moment of distance. An interlude so that things can be tied up again and smooth functioning can resume. A representation of the useful.[3]

But what is it to insert distance into a field of relation if not violence of the highest degree? Whose distance? At what cost? To what ends?

Guattari fights against this at every turn, refusing mediation either in politics or in psychiatry. Schizoanalysis is the proposition, a call for a transversal operation that breaks the pretense of neutrality in the encounter. A therapeutics of transversality. No more triangle. No more transference. Schizoanalysis is the event of the encounter itself, the practice of encountering. To be in the relation is to have been changed by it. What this looked like: a years-long institutional arrangement housed at a clinic called La Borde in the north of France whereby to be in the therapeutic encounter was to live with the effects of encounters in the everyday and to learn from them how to continue to live. Nothing very complicated, really. But infinitely

3 See Erin Manning, *For a Pragmatics of the Useless* (Durham: Duke University Press, 2020) for a more sustained engagement with the concept of the representation of the useful.

complex in its transversality. Because to live in the encounter, to allow ourselves to be changed by it, is to be continuously undone, and to be sensitive to all that comes alive in that undoing.

Who we are is a question that can only really be asked (and answered) by the mediator. The mediator, after all, looks in from outside to tell us how our actions are affecting the world. Without the mediator there is no steady external gaze, no calm interface for the mirroring. That's why "who we are" is always a white question, a question of whiteness, of colonization.

Blackness, write Moten and Harney, is not a thing, or a state (of being). It is the way the doing expresses. It is not a subject, not a person, not a property. It is a field. It is the excess on itself of a body claimed, blackened by hate. Blackness is the celebration of refusing to claim, to be claimed. "Meanwhile, Michael Brown is like another fall and rise through man – come and gone, as irruption and rupture, to remind us not that black lives matter but that black life matters; that the absolute and undeniable blackness of life matters; that this is not a judgment of value but a description of a field of activity that obliterates the worldly distinction between the organic and the inorganic" (Harney and Moten 2021, 49). Blackness is not the simple descriptor of what has been enfleshed. Blackness cannot be mediated into a form imposed (exposed). Blackness is the force of living that exceeds colonization, its accursed share. And in that sense, the wildness of the surround, it too is black. As is the earth.

This is what Guattari means when he entreats us to move from schizoanalysis as a therapeutic-political dispositif, an *agencement* more than an apparatus, a moving-forth of encounterings afield, toward the transversality of what he calls the "three ecologies" (2000). These three ecologies, the mental/conceptual, the environmental, and the social, are the overlap, as I see it, of a commitment to a blackening of the earth, out of the clear.

> ([N]ecessarily European) man, in and as the exception, imposes speciation upon himself, in an operation that extracts and excepts himself from the earth in order to confirm his supposed dominion over it. And just as the earth must be forcefully speciated to be possessed, man must forcefully speciate himself in order to enact this kind of possession. This is to say that racialization is present in the very idea of dominion over the earth; in the very idea and enactment of

> the exception; in the very nuts and bolts of possession-by-improvement. The world is posed as the way to live on the earth as the individual is posed as the way to live in the world. To live in the world as an individual is therefore to be logistic, and to be logistic is to settle into a rhythm that kills, to beat out that rhythm over the undercommon track that keeps (giving away) its own measure. (Harney and Moten 2021, 29)

Scene 7

Guattari wrote *The Three Ecologies* (2000) in what have come to be known as his winter years. The winter years came after a sustained attempt at working with the Green party in the aftermath of the terrible let down of post-1968 politics in France. This attempt to connect to state politics left Guattari with a sour taste. He knew better, of course, than to trust state politics to be a site of transformation. Schizoanalysis had been the wager that there were other ways – that to work "in common," "toward the common," is, ultimately, always to commit to the logic of mediation. In *The Three Ecologies,* he makes a plea to invent new ways of being committed to and involved in the urgent call to transversalize experience, ways that move beyond how the state lays claim to existence:

> In the domain of social ecology there will be times of struggle in which everyone will feel impelled to decide on common objectives and to act 'like little soldiers,' by which I mean like good activists. But there will simultaneously be periods of resingularisation in which individual and collective subjectivities will take their marbles and go home without a thought for collective goals, and in which creative expression as such will take precedence. This new ecosophical logic – and I want to emphasize this point – resembles the manner in which an artist may be led to alter his work after the intrusion of some accidental detail, an event-incident that suddenly makes his initial project bifurcate, making it drift [dériver] far from its previous path, however certain it had once appeared to be. (51, *translation modified*)

There is an echo in this ecosophic call to Moten and Harney:

> Rather than dissipate our preoccupation with how we live and breathe, we need to defend our ways in our persistent practice of them. It's not about taking the streets; it's about how, and about what, we take to the streets. What would it be and what would it mean for us jurisgeneratively to take to the streets, to live in the streets, to gather together another city right here, right now? (2021, 48-49)

Ecosophic logic is a refusal of the clearing, of the ways in which we seek to inhabit the space already colonized. It recognizes the lure, and understands the commitment to change that the gesture of taking the streets embodies. But ecosophic logic asks a different question: what if instead we practiced living by creating new conditions that didn't center us, that didn't inadvertently redeem that central and self-centering figure of man and its mediating logistics? What if we painted into the *dérive* of artfulness's angle on experience? What if we moved at the pace of that accidental detail tangled with the weeds we have been wasting so much time clearing?

Ecosophic logic is an urgent call to refuse the ongoing clearing that denies, decries, and violates the force of blackness in the ongoing genocide of all that resists the count. To refuse does not mean to face and challenge. Frontality, the neurotypical activity par excellence, only cements into place what is already there, what is already claiming the ground of existence. To refuse means to move into the accursed share of life-living twisting in the troubled interstice, to move with that anarchic share of existence that keeps giving life.

For life-living to thrive, life has to be activated at those interstices that exceed man. Life's expression as tangle has to be attuned to from the edges in. Conditions have to be crafted to honor what is not about us. This is what the First Nations in *Barkskins* of course already knew. And for this they were cleared. To see, to feel, what was always already there, to pulse with a force of life-living that cannot be claimed – owed or owned – this was always the crime.

Scene 8

The many years Guattari spent practicing schizoanalysis, which is to say, living at La Borde and encountering, daily, the shape of an existence unmediated, an existence committed, always, to a refusal of normopathy – these are what he takes into the project of the three ecologies.

And it is specifically the orientation of La Borde toward neurodiversity, I believe, that makes it necessary to underscore what he calls the mental, or conceptual ecology as the inflecting force that must, and will, change the contours of the environmental and the social. La Borde taught him this: to skirt the question of the subject leaves the black hole wide open, filled to the brim with neurotypicality, whiteness.

In the sickness that has befallen the earth – the ongoing genocide of all that eludes the count – subjectivity, too, has fallen ill. Replaced by the face of man, given the guise of whiteness in all its logistical powers of mediation, subjectivity has been swallowed, engulfed by the subject. "The main feature of the colonial-capitalistic unconscious is the reduction of subjectivity to its subject's experience" (Rolnik 2017, np). But subjectivity, as Guattari understands it, is nothing other than its ongoing production. It is not the subject. It is the transversal, the emergent unmediated middle, the collectivity that must never be reduced to the one. This is why, for a renewed project of the earth, or as Moten and Harney would have it, for the blackening of the earth – "we are the moving, blackened, blackening earth" (2021, 113) – "it will be a question of literally reconstructing the modalities of 'group-being' [*l'être-en-groupe*], not only through 'communicational' interventions but through existential mutations driven by the motor of subjectivity" (Guattari 2000, 34).

To construct modalities for group-being is a call for an aesthetics of sociality which exceeds the 1+1 of interpersonality. Group-being, or what Guattari refers to as the "group subject" is not countable. The group subject is never the sum of its parts. As solitary as it is multiplicitous, the group subject makes felt how subjectivity is produced in the excess on itself of coming into relation. The group subject is how the more-than of the relational field finds expression. It is the emergent collectivity of an expression of life-living shared (in its accursed excess), expression irreducible to the one, always beyond consensus. Without mediation, the group subject is activated in the renunciation of summing up. To produce the modalities for this excess of existence requires a mutation on existence itself, a mutation that in every sense rethinks subjectivity as a position.

The group subject reminds us that what we produce is never solely ours. We are not simply our-selves. We are fieldings of complex imbrication. Any other account of experience is subjected to mediation, organized by logistics. Anarchival to the core, the production of subjectivity is not an account of a life contained. It is not condensable to something like identity. It is not reducible to the form of the human. It is always more-than, always in movement, a motor or conduit of a worlding.

The production of subjectivity bodies in the same gesture that it refuses to be *a* body, an "individual-in-subjection" (Harney and Moten 2021, 14). That is to say: in the production of subjectivity the bodying is always a being of relation. Always in movement, it does its living in the unlimited exposure that exceeds any body-world separation. Subjectivity is not inside. It is not in me. It is out of me.

> Rather than speak of the 'subject,' we should perhaps speak of components of subjectification, each working more or less on its own. This would lead us, necessarily, to re-examine the relation between concepts of the individual and subjectivity, and, above all, to make a clear distinction between the two. Vectors of subjectification do not necessarily pass through the individual, which in reality appears to be something like a 'terminal' for processes

> that involve human groups, socio-economic ensembles, data-processing machines, etc. Therefore, interiority establishes itself at the crossroads of multiple components, each relatively autonomous in relation to the other, and, if need be, in open conflict. (Guattari 2000, 36)

"That abolition starts with the self" (Harney and Moten 2021, 172).

In the drift, subjectivity's *dérive* is irreducible to the human. Active in the interval of worlds making themselves, subjectivity is never reducible to a subject. The production of subjectivity is the activity of the interstice: vector, not form. Schizoanalysis works at this uneasy juncture. The task of schizoanalysis is not to get between body and world, between-two. Its task is to make way for all that already populates the between, and to agitate, from within the field of relation, orientations already in germ. Fostering the germination, tending the field, schizoanalysis vectors the inflection.

The vectoring requires a subtraction from the open field of all that is still in potentia. Schizoanalysis culls from potential a shape, a way. This excision from process is a subtraction from infinitude to the finite. From the side of infinitude, in the field of immanence, Whitehead calls this activity that sparks a standing out of experience "importance." From the side of finitude, in the field of activity, Whitehead calls it "expression":

> expression is founded on the finite occasion. It is the activity of finitude impressing itself on its environment. Thus it has its origin in the finite; and it represents the immanence of the finite in the multitude of its fellows beyond itself. The two together, namely importance and expression, are witnesses both to the monistic aspect of the universe and to its pluralistic character. Importance passes from the world as one to the world as many; whereas, expression is the gift from the world as many to the world as one. (1968, 20)

Importance and expression function as intensifiers of experience, bringing into activity the singularity of a life that nonetheless continues to carry its anarchic share. In this account, the human is not singled out. There is no externalizing voice, no mediator. Arrows of experience are their own force, importance not a question of what matters to me, but of what actually (but always also in potentia) *makes a difference*.

Importance makes way for precision in experience. That is to say, importance is what fosters a certain specific angle of existence, allowing certain qualities of experience to take precedence over others. We have come to believe that mediation is necessary to parse experience. But as Whitehead emphasizes, the world is always in its own pursuit of amplification. Incessant clearing, colonialism without end, in the afterlife of slavery, results in systems out of kilter. Ecological destruction has finally begun to register, centuries too late. The question of how to bring things into a metastability that is conducive to life-living must involve a reckoning with the deadening force of mediation. We don't need another apology. We need to get out of the way. The blackening of the earth requires the production of something entirely other than me, or you.

Scene 9

The infraface[4] of the three ecologies – "the world as one to the world as many [...] the world as many

---

4 See Erin Manning and Brian Massumi, "Infrafacing," in *Affects, Interface, Event*, eds. Bodil Marie Stavning Thomsen, Jette Kofoed, and Jonas Fritsch (Lancaster and Vancouver: Imbricate!, 2021), 307-326.

to the world as one" (Whitehead 1968, 20) – is *immediating*.[5] Immediation is not the opposite of mediation. Rather, it is the force of a thirdness irreducible to a between-two. Immediation is the more-than, the n+1 that is by necessity n-1, one as many, many as one, the qualitative force of an uncountability that diagonalizes to give rise to what else moves in the relation.

The production of subjectivity is immediating to the degree that it is not produced by something outside itself. Immediating, always at once body and world, its own perspective. That is to say, its angle on existence is not ours, cannot be reduced to us. The production of subjectivity is a making-conceptual of existence. It is an attuning to the deadly violence of the body-world split produced in the wake of the clearing (Sharpe 2016).

There are not three ecologies. There is one ecology multiply intertwined. To get to the potential of what the three ecologies in their transversality offer, the production of subjectivity must be attended to. We have failed each other at the juncture of the production of subjectivity in particular,

---

5 For more on immediation, see *Immediation, Vols 1-2*, eds. Anna Munster, Erin Manning, and Bodil Marie Stavning Thomsen (London: Open Humanities Press, 2019).

and nothing will be possible without that shift. In the words of The Invisible Committee,

> [t]he exhaustion of natural resources is probably much less advanced than the exhaustion of subjective resources, of vital resources, that is afflicting our contemporaries. If so much satisfaction is derived from surveying the devastation of the environment it's largely because this veils the frightening ruin of subjectivities. Every oil spill, every sterile plain, every species extinction is an image of our souls in rags, a reflection of our lack of world, of our intimate impotence to inhabit it. (2014, qtd. in Rolnik 2017)

To become in excess of a person, to activate the conditions for a life-living that worlds in the bodying, is a social and environmental act. The emergent sociality of becoming-environmental never happens through the clearing. It happens in the midst, black flies and all. The production of subjectivity in the transversality of the three ecologies is the way the more-than of nature naturing crafts a sociality ecosophically. A sociality, as Moten and Harney might say, *all incomplete.*

Guattari calls the ecology he associates with

the production of subjectivity "mental." I prefer conceptual, to produce a stronger sense of how the world itself is alive with the movement of thought. A turn to Whitehead brings the two together. For Whitehead, the conceptual share is that excess of experience that tunes the occasion to its potential. All activity in the world has a conceptual share, but it is true to say that some aspects of existence make use of it more emphatically. Whitehead calls this "mentality" (1958, 32-34). Mentality, as in Guattari, is not reducible to the mind. Mentality is the force of existence. It is the world's capacity to exceed itself. All incomplete, the world continuously renews itself.

Scene 10

We don't need to look to some far-off lands: it's already here. Isn't that what Tommy Orange means when he says: "being Indian has never been about returning to the land. The land is everywhere or nowhere" (2018, 11)? The work has already begun.

The accursed share of life-living is too unwieldy, too uncountable, to be mediated. It cannot be governed. This is its potency, but also its fallacy.

The work is not where we've been taught it is. And the tools we need are not the ones we own.

> *a nascent subjectivity*
> *a constantly mutating socius*
> *an environment in the process of being reinvented*
> (Guattari 2000, 68)

The three ecologies are a proposition. They are not a place. To follow the artist-architects Arakawa and Madeline Gins (2002), we might call them an architectural procedure. An architectural procedure is not an architecture. It is a fielding of potential that brings into constellation enabling constraints for the construction of a world. Procedurality is key. An architectural procedure must produce itself propositionally. This means that what emerges will never be a thing, a site. It will undercommon itself into existence, perhaps – as Arakawa and Gins once said, "only making an appearance indirectly" (2002, 14). Because to see-feel it is to have created the conditions for feeling, conditions that were never reducible to a subject as given in advance. The event of the three ecologies is here, in the productive looping of a field of experience that is at once constitutive of its expression and constituted by it. Because when importance and expression meet, it is never at our bidding.

Angular Perspective

Tommy Orange: "We've been moving for a long time, but the land moves with you like memory. An Urban Indian belongs to the city, and cities belong to the earth. Everything here is formed in relation to every other living and nonliving thing from the earth. All our relations" (2018, 11). Buildings, freeways, cars, Orange insists, "are they not of the earth?" (11). "Being Indian has never been about returning to the land. The land is everywhere or nowhere" (11).

Nature: the force that moves through us. Nature: not "a" place, but a quality of experience that worlds.

Simple Location

A nature, an indefinite and yet singular force that moves us into being. *A* nature, a parastratum, a textured transversality. *A* nature, not *the* nature, not natureculture with nature always on the side of the primitive, the prelinguistic, the land: no sequestering of nature "out there," no assumption that nature can be located, contoured, framed, once and for all.

But first: simple location. Simple location is the belief, deeply held within Western lineages of thought, that nature is "composed of permanent things, namely bits of matter, moving about in space which otherwise is empty" (Whitehead 1968, 128). Nature as the empty vessel through which culture moves. Nature as that which contains matter, movement reduced to a property of preexisting form.

When matter is understood as the substrate of nature's expression, the presupposition is that movement is added from without. What moves is not the world in co-composition but the objects in it, mobilized by external forces. This presupposes that space and time are external to experience: we enter into them. This Kantian account of spacetime reinforces the acculturation of matter in the logic of locatedness, of site. What matters is not how things collide in an ecological interplay. What matters is the epistemological evaluation of a count already presupposed. Alfred

North Whitehead's critique of simple location contests this view. It is a refusal of the notion that matter is somehow "self-sufficient with the simple location of the region which it occupies" (1968, 139).

A disembodied account of matter "taking place" in nature suggests that matter is a simple fact, "just there, in that region where it is" (Whitehead 1968, 139). This extracts experience from the field, making it individual. To reduce experience to the individual, to say matter is "just there," is to posit an account devoid of relation, empty of ecology.

Experience is never individual in the Whiteheadian account. It is cosmological. Ecology must be understood in this cosmological philosophy as relation itself. Experience is how the world shifts into a shape, and how that shape has concern for the field. Experience as ecology means concern for the field is never reducible to "my" concern. That would return us to nature overcoded by culture. Concern for the field is attunement to the singularity of how nature makes itself felt, how it *matters*.

What matters in the story of matter simply located is not matter but the external valuation of reason over ecology. In this humanist logic, whiteness prevails: power is held by those who preside over the count.[6] The culture-nature binary propelled by the overcoding of nature by culture requires that movement extract itself from experience. Matter remains inert.

A process philosophical account of nature begins in the mattering itself. Movement matters. Indeed, everything matters. “Any local agitation shakes the whole universe” (Whitehead 1968, 138).

6 For a more detailed account of whiteness in the context of the colonial effects of simple location (particularly in relation to neurotypicality), see Erin Manning, *For a Pragmatics of the Useless* (Durham: Duke University Press, 2020). Whiteness is also at work in the above plea from Orange that his Indigeneity not be refused due to a lack of “land” knowledge. “We know the sound of the freeway better than we do rivers, the howl of distant trains better than wolf howls, we know the smell of gas and freshly wet concrete and burned rubber better than we do the smell of cedar or sage or even fry bread – which isn’t traditional, like reservations aren’t traditional, but nothing is original, everything comes from something that came before, which was once nothing. Everything is new and doomed. We ride buses, trains, and cars across, over, and under concrete plains” (2018, 11). The coupling of Indigeneity with land (reservations) serves only to bolster the nature-culture binary, keeping Indigeneity on the side of nature (without culture).

Nature

A nature is a moving field, actualized through the quality of its everchanging expression. The indefinite force of movement-moving is known through the difference it makes, not the location it stakes. *A* nature, in continuity with Gilles Deleuze's *a* life,[7] the force of life-living that exceeds the shape of *this* life,[8] pulsing with the bare activity of movement in germ.[9] Matter matters. Agitation is "fused into its environment" (Whitehead 1968, 138). "The environment enters into the nature of

7 See Gilles Deleuze "Immanence: A Life," in *Pure Immanence: Essays on a Life* (New York: Zone Books, 2005), 25-33.

8 In *Always More Than One: Individuation's Dance* (Durham: Duke University Press, 2013), I write at length about the concept of life-living: "Life is always about a double-capture – on the one hand, it is the force of life-living that exceeds this or that life, and on the other, it is the monadic event of a singular set of conditions in momentary collusion. Life is always between. [...] Life is life-living, in act, replete with the indefinable force of a life coursing through it. Life is a complex of feeling, an ecology not reducible to its data, to its content or its form-takings. Life is the plurality of becoming as felt, a plurality not of many parts – this would place the plural below the category of being – but a plurality at the very level of becoming, a multiplicity in act" (22).

9 On bare activity, see Brian Massumi, *Ontopower: War, Powers, and the State of Perception* (Durham: Duke University Press, 2015).

each thing" (138).

The field is agitated by all that moves it. This is not to say that the agitation is perceptible all the way down. Or, to put it differently, not all perception can be reduced to us, to *our* view of the world. The shaking of the universe is felt in the most minute of ways not *by* us, but *with* us. What is experienced as world, as body, is the effect of force taking form, immanent movement expression. "The distant effects are minute, but they are there" (Whitehead 1968, 138). To conceive of such minute alterations in existence requires a shift in perspective: perspective is the angle of the universe under changing relations. Perspective is an orientation toward intensification that takes "us" with it.

A nature is movement. In the act. "It is nonsense to conceive of nature as a static fact, even for an instant devoid of duration. There is no nature apart from transition, and there is no transition apart from temporal duration. This is the reason why the notion of an instant of time, conceived as a primary simple fact, is nonsense" (Whitehead 1968, 152).

A nature: the expression of all that moves (us), the more-than of life's sited expression.

Actuality

In process philosophy, actual occasions are what express experience. An actual occasion is a grasp of mattering that multiplies the universe's perspective. An occasion is of indefinite scale, magnitude not its concern. An occasion is what occasions, what makes itself *actually* felt in experience. It is an event, in the way Deleuze and Guattari conceive the term (1987).

To come into itself as such, an occasion of experience must exclude what cannot be consolidated to its monadic expression. An occasion will be affected by what it eliminates, however, despite the elimination not actualizing. In this way, an occasion of experience carries potential even while it excludes it from *actually* participating in the consolidation of what will become the lived expression of what has been prehended.[10]

When an actual occasion fully becomes itself, when it satisfies itself, it perishes. A half second, a milisecond, an epoch. What matters is that it passes, that it is transient, despite its monadic character. What remains of it in its passing is

---

10 For a more detailed account of negative prehension, see Erin Manning, "For a Pragmatics of the Useless," in *For a Pragmatics of the Useless* (Durham: Duke University Press, 2020), 15-31.

not the occasion as such, but the ways in which it agitated the universe.

The perishing of the occasion leaves potential in the world. This potential, a field of relation agitated by all that comes to be, is what Whitehead calls the extensive continuum. Despite its allusion to space, the extensive continuum is not space or spacetime. It is a field of *potentia* that, when taken up by an actualizing occasion, produces spacetime. The extensive continuum is a nexus of virtual expressions for life-living.

To resist turning the extensive continuum into an ideal form, it is necessary to recognize that the world is not *actually* made of the extensive continuum. The world is made of actual occasions. But since the occasions are forever perishing, the extensive continuum cannot but be alive with the minor matterings of all that has come to actual expression. This naturing of nature can be felt as a thresholding of actuality and potential. Not a body yet – a bodying, a mattering. "The continuum is present in each actual entity, and each actual entity pervades the continuum" (1978, 67). Process culminates in actualization, but process can never be fully actualized – the potential that courses through it "continuums" it. In the texture of the relational field, actualization is an inflection, a vector.[11] Despite carrying the form of the expression, this vector is but an orientation in a thickly textured field of process. In the inflection that is actualization we have a peaking, an intensification, of all that stirs.

Naturing is an act of experience. Much has been discarded for something to emerge just as it is, a something that will now affect how other somethings can become what they will become. This orientation on a becoming is what Whitehead calls perspective. The how of an occasion becoming is replete with all that potentially moves through it. "The many become one, and are increased by one" (Whitehead 1978, 21).

The many that become one are the potentials subtracted into a unity. The one that increases is the gift the occasion has made to experience. Of course this may be a poison gift. To change the world is not necessarily good. That the many become one is simply to state a bald fact: to come to be is to have shifted the conditions of what was by subtracting from the welter a singular expression of existence.

11 For more on architecture, site, and inflection, see Bernard Cache, *Earth Moves: The Furnishing of Territories* (Cambridge: MIT Press, 1995).

Whitehead writes: "The extensive continuum is that general relational element in experience whereby the actual entities [occasions] experienced, and that unit experience itself, are united in the solidarity of one common world" (1978, 72). When Whitehead speaks of a "common world" in relation to the many and the one, what is common is that it acts, that it expresses, that it changes and moves. That it is one or common is necessary for its being, at the core, different. That is to say, differential relations are what power this so-called unity. Any other solution would require an external force directing the world, a transcendent power. What moves the world is how it comes into relation: difference without separability (Ferreira da Silva, 2016).

Édouard Glissant writes: "Difference is not what separates us. It is the elementary particle of all relation. It is through difference that what I call Relation works" (2010, 91, *my translation*). The unity of its universe is the oneness of relation. This oneness of relation is differential – every shift alters the whole, reorienting it in the interplay of existence, thereby shifting all valuations of what counts. That is to say, experience cannot be externally measured by dividing it into parts. Experience is the eruption of difference that necessitates new forms of valuation at every turn.

A nature is a call for a differential attunement to the more-than that courses through life-living. In the Whiteheadian vocabulary, it is an engagement with the force of the continuum that carries it to expression, a force that extends into the nexus of occasions where it continues to modulate what comes to be. "[N]ature is never complete. It is always passing beyond itself. This is the creative advance of nature" (Whitehead 1978, 289).

Perspective

How the universe moves through the occasion refers to "what the universe is for that entity either in the way of accomplishment or in the way of potentiality" (Whitehead 1968, 66). Whitehead calls it "the perspective of the universe for that entity" (66). "For example, these are the perspectives of the universe for the number three, and for the colour blue, and for any one definite occasion of realized fact" (66). The perspective of the universe for an occasion "arises from the sense of positive achievement within the finite, combined with the sense of modes of infinitude stretching beyond each finite fact. This infinitude is required by each fact to express its necessary relevance beyond its own limitations. It expresses a perspective of the universe" (1968, 78-79).

A perspective of the universe that travels through the occasion of experience puts perspective in the event rather than in the subject. There is no external subject here that could be excised from the occasion. *A* nature is not subject. It is event. Perspective is how the event comes into its actualization, not how "I" see it.

Subject, for Whitehead, is never pregiven. It is composed: of the occasion, carried by a perspective that forms around it as it comes to be.

The grasp – the prehension – that occasions an event is spurred by feeling. The feeling is not felt by a subject. The subject is made by the feeling. "Feeling is the agent which reduces the universe to its perspective for fact" (Whitehead 1968, 10). Fact is the potential actualizing. "It follows that in every consideration of a single fact there is the suppressed presupposition of the environmental coördination requisite for its existence. This environment, thus coördinated, is the whole universe in its perspective to the fact" (9). Fact is activity consolidated. Perspective is the angle on that consolidation from within its coming to be.

The angle on consolidation gives us *a* nature. Perspective is not point of view so much as emergent orientation in the feel. "[P]erspective is the outcome of feeling; and feeling is graded by the sense of interest as to the variety of its differentiations" (10). Perspective is the expression of feeling felt. Perspective is the angle of that motoring, an angle expressive of a differential field of relation.

Perspective has nothing to do with vision here. It is feeling-felt, in the orienting toward what accentuates experience, inflecting it. Perspective: the angle that reshapes the field.

Eduardo Viveiros de Castro writes of Amerindian perspectivism in ways that texture Whitehead's account. "Amerindian ontological perspectivism proceeds along the lines that the point of view creates the subject" (Viveiros de Castro 1998, 6). In the Amerindian cosmology, perspectivism similarly refuses simple location: "the opposition between being and becoming, in Amerindian thought, is not equivalent to that between 'structure' and 'process' (much less to that between 'essence' and 'appearance' or 'reality' and 'representation'), but rather to that between univocal identity and plurivocal multiplicity" (Viveiros de Castro 2015, 288). Here, perspectivism refers to a process of becoming that occurs between humans and animals whereby an emergent reconsolidation of experience recalibrates the species line: a jaguar in a predatory relationship to the human will become the human in that particular relation. The status of the body is emergent in perspectival orientation. Human is not baseline, naturing-nature is.

In the metamorphosis of emergent relation, the transformation is not from one thing to another, from jaguar to human, or human to jaguar, as though there could be a clear starting and endpoint that occurs on a flat, simply located ground of existence. Rather, the becoming is a reorientation of the whole field of experience, a new perspective, a relational act. Becoming is movement of ground, angle on grasp. "Transformation or becoming is a 'quality,' not a process – it is an instantaneous shift of perspectives, or rather the entangled, non-decidable coexistence of two perspectives, each hiding the other in order to appear, like those figure-ground reversals we are familiar with, or like the flipping over of the front and back halves of the 'two-sided species'" (Viveiros de Castro 2015, 288). The coming into perspective is the act that natures beings. "In the act of becoming what changes is not the subject, but the world" (287).

Viveiros de Castro calls this approach multinaturalism. Multinaturalism refuses multiculturalism as the leading motif of diversity. Enough of culture's imposition on nature! Multinaturalism recognizes the differential in and of nature, its intrinsic capacity for difference. "Hence, where our modern, anthropological multiculturalist ontology is founded on the mutual implication of the unity of nature and the plurality of cultures, the Amerindian conception would suppose a spiritual unity and a corporeal diversity – or, in other words, one 'culture,' multiple 'natures'" (2015, 59). Multinaturalism refutes the kind of relativism typically found in accounts of "diversity" in multiculturalism, accounts that always return to individual perspective in simple location.

The Amerindian multinatural perspective is an account of a singular-indefinite *a* nature. Nature is not generalized here, overlaid by culture's Enlightenment principles. Nature is the differential force of all that comes to be, potential and actualization interwoven. Nature is *how* the world expresses itself.

A nature is both absolute and indefinite. It is absolute in that its bodying expresses a character of existence that matters, here-now. It is indefinite in that it carries the continuum, the perspective of the universe always an immanent orientation in what comes to be. This immanent orientation keeps it in the moving, in the differentiating, in a becoming of continuity (not a continuity of becoming) (Whitehead 1978, 35). Each actualization shifts the conditions of nature's naturing, potentially reorienting.

The indefiniteness of *a* nature is also its impersonality. That is to say, nature persons, persons don't have a nature. And in the personing, what is amplified always contains an angle of incompleteness: "nature is never complete. It is always passing beyond itself" (Whitehead 1978, 289). This incompleteness is naturing nature's impersonality, its modality of excess on any notion of stability, of identity.

Creativity

A nature is creative in its potential. This potential is expressed in what Whitehead calls "contrast" (1967, 216). Contrast is the felt reverberation of potential in the actual, the quality, perceived in the relation, of a backgroundingforegrounding.[12]

12 For a more detailed exploration of backgroundingforegrounding, also in terms of an ethics of relation, see Erin Manning, "backgroundingforegrounding" in *For a Pragmatics of the Useless* (Durham: Duke University Press, 2020), 103-113.

Think pulse, in overlap, the incessant push and pull of what anchors itself in perspective and what flows through it as potential.

The danger is to invite the substantive to return, to welcome matter as simple location, to solidify a personing of the subject as the central perceiver. These are the fallacies of misplaced concreteness. Creativity dies under these conditions.

A relational texturing is always a movement. In the backgroundingforegrounding, what appears is contoured by what has just retreated. To reduce this to a visual image would be to flatten it: care must be taken to allow the expression of difference to retain its relational interplay. A Whiteheadian perspectivism is thick with feeling, less front-back than zigzag.

Whitehead speaks of this in terms of the private and the public, referring to the ways in which occasions face their absolute actualization and their immanent relations, both-and, at one and the same time (1978, 289-90). When an occasion of experience actualizes, it carries into its consolidation the quality of expression that makes it what it is. This quality of expression – a redness, say – is private to the degree that its reference can be traced directly to the prehension that oriented it in just this way. And yet it is public in the very same gesture because it is of the world. Redness is already a perspective of the universe, offering itself to the world's incipient grasp. In its accomplishment – its satisfaction, as Whitehead would say – redness as expressed just this way has introduced a singular quality to a world reshaping itself around it while pulling the world back into its inheritance. Future-pastness grasped in the specious present of this singular occasion.

The vacillation, in and of the occasion, between the public and the private, its backgrounding-foregrounding, makes contrast the protagonist. That is to say, nothing emerges into the world that does not carry, in one and the same gesture, the mattering of a form-taking, and the incorporeal that runs through it. "Of it, but not it. Real, material, but incorporeal. Inseparable, coincident, but disjunct" (Massumi 2021, 5). Incorporeal materialism: "the felt reality of relation" (17).

Certainly, the more-than of incorporeal materialism can be muted, and it often is. *A* nature is often reduced to *the* nature, to simple location and its fallacy of misplaced concreteness. Hard and fast facts are mobilized to overpower the nuance of a nature naturing. Bodies are hardened to their shells, and placed on an unmoving earth. That doesn't stop the process of the world making itself, however. It just mutes its power of differentiation. This power is the force of feeling that motors experience, a force always in excess of the forms things take.

"The body, as the site of differentiating perspective, must be differentiated to the highest degree in order to completely express it" (Viveiros de Castro 2015, 265). "Far from regaining a concreteness, to think the body in movement thus means accepting the paradox that there is an incorporeal dimension *of the body*" (Massumi 2021, 5). This excess of differentiation is the expression of *a* nature's infinite complexity. "This would make the incorporeal something like a phase-shift of the body in the usual sense, but not one that comes after it in time. It would be a conversion or unfolding of the body contemporary to its every move. Always accompanying. Fellow-traveling dimension of the same reality" (5).

A nature: body-worlding.

A nature: incorporeal materialism.

A nature: "the body as an implication of the very concept of perspective" (Viveiros de Castro 2015, 37).

Concern

Perspective is another way to express concern for how relation fields. "Each occasion is an activity of concern" (Whitehead 1968, 167). Concern: the motor of feeling's carrying of occasion from force to form. "It is the conjunction of transcendence and immanence" (167).

The occasion's concern for consolidation is not a concern for form. It is a concern for the more-than of an incorporeal materialism, a concern for all that exceeds the form actualization will take. "The occasion is concerned, in the way of feeling and aim, with things that in their own essence lie beyond it; although these things in their present functions are factors in the concern of that occasion" (167).

Concern animates the process of creativity in the contrasting field. It is the conduit for the carrying across thresholds of what matters, incorporeally. If actualization always involves subtraction, concern is the care for what is left over, for the more-than that cannot in itself be consolidated.

Concern, with the quality of a minor gesture,[13] motors the edges of what cannot quite conform.

---

13 For an account of the minor gesture, see Erin Manning, *The Minor Gesture* (Durham: Duke University Press, 2016).

Buoyed not by an outside constituency but by an inner logic recrafted for each inflection of the field, concern attunes the occasion to how it matters.

Objective Immortality

When an occasion perishes, its form perishes along with it, but there remains what Whitehead calls "objective immortality" (1978, 137). What has affected the world by actualizing is never known again as such, but an edge of its being remains as *potentia* to feed-forward through future occasions. This is how the relational complex expresses itself across epochs.

In this account of antecedence and its inheritances, the pull of past occasions is felt in their quality, not their actuality: "The only intelligible doctrine of causation is founded on the doctrine of immanence. Each occasion presupposes the antecedent world as active in its own nature" (Whitehead 1968, 165). The medium of the occasion, its naturing, is coloured by the force of what immortally makes up its immanent surrounds. *A* nature is born of those edgings into occurrence.

Objective immortality relies on what Whitehead calls "contemporary independence." Contemporary independence, he says, provides "elbow-room within the Universe" (1967, 195). Two unique occasions are never mappable on each other. Without contemporary independence of actual occasions, the universe would be gridlocked – all would connect to all, no cracks, no play. Experience would be reduced to piles of simple locations seeking precedence. Objective immortality is a reminder that experience is not reducible to any notion of interactivity – to any form-to-form encounter: the relational web of experience is composed of the hum of a world in-formation. The past cannot be carried fully-formed into the present. It comes with the pulse of its in-formation, with the intensity of all that made it what it was. But it doesn't come as "it-self." The force-of-form of existence making itself is always in excess of the shape it took.

Contemporary independence means that there is no matrix whereupon the occasioning rests, no continuous line of experience. No continuity of becoming, as Whitehead's refrain goes, but a becoming of continuity, a reshaping in the encounter (1978, 35). A simple account of cause and effect as the matrix of existence is obliterated in this account of experience. Each movement matters. Each movement differs. What textures the relational web of existence is not the actual, but what reverberates in the contrast of its backgroundingforegrounding.

Objective immortality is the fresh air of the system, the potential for new operations casting new angles on the world. For there to be difference, something has to take. For something to take, it has to differentiate itself.

In one and the same movement, something and everything expresses. Something is the expression of difference through which the consolidation of experience in this actual occasion will divert from existing modalities, even if only in the most minute of ways. Everything is the quality of concern that accompanies the comings into relation of the field of experience expressing itself. Something and everything in each occasion, in excess of each occasion. The something and everything is the one and many of Whitehead's "the many become one and are increased by one" (1978, 21). There is never simply something: something always carries the echo of all it could become in the agitation of everything in its perspectival focus on that something. *A* nature lives here, in that contrast.

Wonder

Process philosophy is activist philosophy (Massumi 2011, 1-28). It asks of the world that it participate in the creativity of its potential. This is not a human-driven cosmology. The force of transformation is never in what I have elsewhere called the volition-intentionality-agency triad.[14] The field of *a* nature is not reducible to me, to my agency, to my volition. It is *movement*. What moves experience is not a preexisting subject. What matters is the concern for the field – its own immanent orienting.

Perspective is immanent to the event, and in that qualitative orientation, an emergent field beckons. Wonder lives here. "We are in the world and the world is in us" (Whitehead 1968, 165).

---

14 For a more detailed account of the volition-intentionality-agency triad and its commitment to neurotypicality, see "Carrying the Feeling," in *The Minor Gesture* (Durham: Duke University Press, 2016), 131-164.

Catch an Incline

To begin with black sociality – rather than to produce a Black subject from the perspective of the world as given – is to refuse, as Tina Campt might say, the assumption that all worlds produced and entered into are White:

> **refusal**: a rejection of the status quo as livable and the creation of possibility in the face of negation i.e. a refusal to recognize a system that renders you fundamentally illegible and unintelligible; the decision to reject the terms of diminished subjecthood with which one is presented, using negation as a generative and creative source of disorderly power to embrace the possibility of living otherwise. (2019, np)

Living otherwise begins in the relational field, a field replete with the force of what is still in the forming. This fierce commitment to other ways of living is, in one and the same gesture, a repudiation of what Saidiya Hartman calls "the burdened individuality of freedom" and an affirmation of modes of existence activated in the interstices (1997, 9).

Here, a logic of approximation of proximity leads the way. Process philosophy, the study of the relational imbrications through which worlds form themselves, echoes with the call for a sociality that is black in its ethico-aesthetic commitment to worlding. A logic of approximation of proximity recognizes the gaps, and moves through them, interested in the differential that produces complexity. The overlap is not seamless. The seam textures the encounter.

To catch an incline is to already be in the midst of the minor sociality that angles, in advance of any other ways of being, toward what Édouard Glissant might call an aesthetics of the earth (1997, 151). Black sociality is the conduit, the orientation, that angles otherwise, bringing the earth's necessities into focus, the impersonality of the minor everywhere active in the lively syncopations it provokes.

•

In an aesthetics of the earth, the balance shifts toward the relational field. It is from the field itself, in the relation, that modes of existence emerge, and it is in collaboration with the field that an ethos of participation with the world is practiced (Glissant 1997). In a celebration of this logic of the "included middle," a different account must be given of how difference is made, which is to say, how we come into the becoming of our ethico-aesthetic engagement with the world (Massumi 2014; Massumi 2021).

In a process philosophical cosmology, which is to say, in approximation of proximity with an aesthetic sociality of blackness, the question of existence's persistence stages a core problem. How are we made? And what makes the field through which we recognize ourselves?

In abeyance of any concept of the self-serving individual who leads existence, in departure from the colonial narrative that places the subject – whiteness – in advance of the world, outside looking in, the account here given begins not in the personal but in the world. The personal, that edge of recognition that sidles "I," is not the beginning of the story. It is a certain echo of its continuance, a feel for persistence, an infra-recognizability, but it *is* not.

Before there is form, and between any notion of consolidation, there is process, open field.

This open field is made of all that is in germ, that ontopowerful[15] field of relation. Being emerges from cut, from the fissure of worlds remaking themselves. That is to say: any consolidation of a modality of existence is produced through a tension in the field that moves it into reshaping. We are made from that subtraction of potential into a recalibration, into act, that, in the same gesture, remakes the world.

To recalibrate into act, there has to be a share of givenness. Something doing. The world's immanent agitations produce the orientation toward cusping out of which being – the being of relation – irrupts. The cut that sparks the recalibration is a necessity for something to "take," to be known. This something is not yet being. It is the quality on-its-way, a becoming, a tending toward form.

This tending toward form takes the shape of all that brought it into the form it takes. It pulls the world with it, carrying all that sidled its process of becoming. As we become, we become (with) the world.

This account of how a form feels itself into being from the force of the field reminds us that we are

15 On ontopower, see Brian Massumi, *Ontopower: War, Powers, and the State of Perception* (Durham: Duke University Press, 2015).

not the sole doers in our process of becoming. We are the collaborators, and in that collaboration we are the carriers of all that fostered our singular becoming. What emerges moves in the feel of that collaboration, carrying with it the tensions and cuts and fissures that brought it to "it-self." "We" are (in) the momentum, (in) the abyss, of the crack, to use Bayo Akomolafe's words (2021b). In the cross-current of accounts of blackness and what it can do, this is what is heard: the world is made in the cracks, not "my" world, not the world in "my" image, but a worlding that dances me into it. "More than my damn self" (Harney and Moten 2021, 45). Blackness as the ungovernable proposition that life begins elsewhere and does its work otherwise than from the perspective of that subject looking in, organizing the world into his image. Blackness as cracked becoming in the atemporality of the most ontopowerful of events: the being of relation.

The givenness that moves the world into act is itself activity. Movement all the way down. What this means: we are made of activity. We are made of the cracks that open us onto being. In the Whiteheadian cosmology, it is the concept of decision that activates this schism that pulls activity out of the immanent valuation of the world in flux (1978, 88). Not world and then human, but vectored activity decisionally become-human.

Whether we call it decision or simply crack, what matters is that what motors us into being is the field's relational complexity subtracted into reorientation. The act of becoming (human) must always be the carrying of this cleave, the crack that opens us into our difference while it holds – in the gap – all that exceeds us. This being of relation that we are is activated in the cusp of worlds reorienting. We are worlded into being through a vectoring of the field. This vectoring cuts process to activate the angle on existence we come to know as what came to pass. The movement of our being is the becoming of the world. There is no separation, only conduit and cut.

Decision here is not a conscious action performed by a pre-existing subject. Decision is its own motivator. The future anterior is how the living is felt: the world moves us into being in the afteraffect of the world's coming to form. We are bodied in the affective tonality of a world expressed through us.

It is common to learn that what matters (and how we matter) happens through the agency of a subject's decisional orientation. It is typical to learn that it is personal agency that gives us power. Blackness teaches us otherwise. Decisioning ourselves into act does not mean that there is no role to play in the activity of living. It means that the playing out of life-living occurs from the middling where earth and body meet. Life is the interplay of the qualities of existence that in-form it. Life is the practice of creating the conditions for that interplay.

The crack that fissures the processual field is a bodying that yields an aesthetic potential. Life is that aesthetic potential, angling itself into shape. Blackness lives that angle, an angular sociality that irrupts from the cracks, its quality of existence taking us into the interstices.

There is no separation between who we are and how we world.

The angular sociality of a worlding that becomes us is a minor sociality – its inclination angles existence toward the sideways tendencies of attention decentered. We are not the directors of this existence-sidling. Accompaniments in the relational field of worlds decisioning themselves into act, we participate. This is the queer inclination of an aesthetics of the earth.

The impersonal lurks here.

•

> My blackness is a roaming principle, a geological force uncovering the otherwise, a departure from convenient algorithms, a fierce conjuring in a language so secret that the words themselves do not realize they are part of the spell. My blackness is an invitation to the sensuousness of the pothole, to the hospitality of the crack in the wall. My blackness is what happens when loss touches itself, when a people is brought to the edge of apocalyptic Atlantic waters, and still carry a strange hope. My blackness is the creolized promiscuity at the borderlands of goodness. My blackness is the miraculous undoing of identity. (Akomolafe 2021b, np)

•

In the angling of sociality, black living endures (Nyong'o 2018). But this endurance is not an endurance of the (time)line. It is an endurance folded, time on the bias. Not identity, not form. Being of relation.

What is a persistence that does not individualize, that doesn't seek self-recognition? What is persistence that never succumbs to "it-self"? What is persistence that is born of the crack, pulsed into act in a movement that refuses the separability of the me-you, body-earth?

Whitehead speaks of a "thread of personal order" (1978, 107). Personal order, the persistence, in the event, of a certain infra-recognizability, is how Whitehead addresses a tendency toward stability in the field of experience. Counter to the decisional cleave, personal order is the carrying-over, the spread, in time, of existence's overlay.

A personal order has a personality to the degree that its carry-over resonates in the fold of time. But it is not reducible to a person or to an object. It does not belong to the logic of a self. Personal order is the perseverance of a tonality, a qualitative ongoingness in the event. Personal order is the reminder that no activity erupts from a vacuum and no mode of existence can be excised from the complex ways it carries the world, and is carried by it. The question is: what kind of endurance is at work, and what is given shape by the endurance?

What carries-over is not the form things take. What carries-over is the intensity of a shaping.

This intensity has a character. What endures, in the event, is the character or personality of valuation that flows into it. The personality of valuation is more than a person – it is the quality of personing that runs through the event. The personality of valuation is the qualitative angle through which the occasion lives its continuing *across*.

The personality of valuation colours the event. Affective in its valence, the valuation is a cast, an allure, that shades the event into a timeline that both times it and from which it overflows. Activity and value in mutual inclusion, the force of the carrying-over becomes indiscernible from "it-self." The personing is made of the personality of valuation that carries it.

The "it-self" of personal order is lost in the layerings of so many carryings. It is conduit.

This conduit is in-time to the degree that its persistence is lived, here-now. But it is also out-of-time, in overflow of any and all actuality. A tinge of immortality moves with it, if by "immortality" we understand the quality of experience that exceeds actualization yet continues to make a difference across it (Whitehead 1941).

The immortality of personal order is impersonal. That is to say: what endures in experience is impersonal – it cannot be reduced to any notion of identity or to any limited notion of the person. There is no containment of personality here as identity purports to do. What endures in the personality of valuation is not the self-same but the force of the carryings-over: the impersonality of affect.

The impersonal cuts across personal order in the shape of time bent. Angling into the differential of valuation's spread, it is never known as such. Without a form, the impersonality of affect takes the shape of the value that inflects it. This impersonality that acts as intercessor to personal order is not a being. It is a throb in time, a hesitancy of the line, felt across an uneasy array of differential acts.

The impersonal is the biggest threat to identity, to the individual and all that is reduced to form by the imposition of time on a line. Where identity claims a given form, relying on that form to do the work of staging difference, the impersonal is nothing but angles, nothing but inflections. The impersonal *is* not in any normal sense of being. The impersonal is relation of non-relation, that carrier of existence that functions only from the middle and remains there. The included middle – the associated milieu, as Gilbert Simondon might say (1995) – is not between-two. The middle is the hospitality of the crack, the cut that opens expression to its outside.

Inclination can only be impersonal, leaning as it does on its uneasy surrounds, forming them in the process, while being formed by them. Valuation has this imprint on experience, lending it not a monumentality but a shade, a slant. When personing edges toward the inclination of valuation, a hesitation troubles actualization. Time stutters, the occasion impersonalized by a durational fold felt in the crook of its givenness. There is no I here, no straight (time)lines.

•

That blackness lives here means this: blackness is the inclination of existence's potential, the aesthetic yield that expresses, in force, not form, the more-than of existence. This minor sociality is not reducible to a person. To reduce it to an identity would be to limit its yield, culling the impersonality of the valuation that flows through it. This is how I hear Rizvana Bradley and Denise Ferreira da Silva's refusal to reduce the aesthetic to the known: "Black Aesthetics is an utterance that, in its immanent derangement of modernity's grammar, marks and is marked by the art of passage without coordinates or arrival, the art of life in departure" (2021, np).

The impersonality of affect reminds us that the "autonomy" of affect[16] does not imply an externality. Affect is an imbrication, an alongsideness that angles activity. Affect is the impersonal force that opens activity to the expression of its feel, in the feel. The danger of personal order is not that it exists but that its endurance be understood in the logic of the (time)line. Personal order's endurance lives in the interplay of decision and the field it opens up, a field we grow out of – the being of relation. What is carried-across is this interplay.

In the interplay, what is made felt is not a unity. A unity has the feel of a hardened form. Unity has no perspective of the universe. Its contours hardened, it cannot let the world in. What is carried-over is the force of the one-many, the more-than-one that reverberates in the exuberant proclamation, back to Akomolafe, that "my blackness is the miraculous undoing of identity," "my" catapulted into all that differs within it. Despite consistency, it reverberates.

16 See "The Autonomy of Affect" in Brian Massumi, *Parables for the Virtual: Movement, Affect, Sensation, Twentieth Anniversary Edition* (Durham: Duke University Press, 2021), 25-48. See especially Massumi's "Preface to the Twentieth Anniversary Edition," xi-xxxi.

Reverberation cracks. Unstable, the first tendency is to find purchase. A temptation: startle into I. A proposition: find a ledge, make a body in the reach. Catch the incline.

Catching the incline angles existence into an intuiting modality. A slanted *I* gives way to a new shape. A crack opens. Below consciousness, the world meets a body obliquely. Impersonality spills across its surfacing. The world tips. "We perceive things where they are, perception puts us at once into matter, is impersonal, and coincides with the perceived object" (Deleuze 1991, 25). I loses its balance.

It is often a temptation to return to that straight I, "the hegemony of the vertical" (Albright 2017, 64)[17] as though there were a beginning, as though the I could guarantee a starting point. The thing is, there is no straight I. There is only the imposition of its legibility through continued centerings of it by whiteness, by neurotypicality, by colonial

17 See also Adeyemi (2019): "The 90° angles of Man (and the related concepts of Human, Subject, and Citizen) were stabilized by the angularities of black to and as ground: in the back-breaking 30°of repetitive agricultural work, the psychological 70° of subservient tending forward with downcast eyes, the sharp shifts between 100° and 110° taken on with each whiplash, the 180° of the dead body, the 0° of '*Cum sup terr*' (Hartman 2008:1)."

logics that keep me in the account of all beginnings. We are not identities in a world of objects. We are the subtractions worlds become when we coincide with the shapes things take. We are cusps of activity and value, impersonally forging existences at the interstices of worlds in the making. "[A]ll our false problems derive from the fact that we do not know how to go beyond experience toward the conditions of experience, toward the articulations of the real, and rediscover what differs in kind in the composites that are given to us and on which we live" (Deleuze 1991, 26).

The real carries the impersonal force of what cusps. It is the affective force of value's effect on activity. The real is the feel of the fissure of experience that cusps valuation where it is in act. Here, the one and the many coincide, their limit-conditions in relational fold. Along the inflection of this untimely line, what emerges is a discordant multiplicity. This multiplicity feels experience into resonance, its affective valence the force of a lure for a shape of actuality that carries the complexity of worlds bodying. The route of this inflection is durational, its line decisionally forked toward paths as yet unformed.

"Duration," Deleuze writes, reading Bergson, "is the most contracted degree of matter, matter the most dilated degree of duration" (1991, 93, *translation modified*). Time is not a line and matter is not an object. Time is the spread of the act's affect on existence. Time is the feel of how the act made a difference. Matter is the actualization of that difference. In the timing of the act, the act's given time, time folds into perspective, its angle making the world resonate in just this way, now. The inclination of this act has a vitality. Bergson calls it "élan vital" (1907).

Élan vital is the affective turn the world takes when it folds the many into one, and the one into many. Time's totality is felt here as pressure, as rhythm. Creativity is made at this interstice.

The pulse of creativity socializes the world into act. The time-signature of this socialization carries a certain hesitation. "There is an efficacity, a positivity of time, that is identical to a 'hesitation' of things, and in this way, to creation in the world" (Deleuze 1991, 105). The divergent lines of experience that time existence hesitate a quality of life into being. This hesitation – the pulse of valuation in activity – trembles the world into the quality of a certain indecision. This in-decision is not a counter to the decisional force that cracks the world into act. It is an in-decision of the act's own certainty as regards how it times experience. The in-decision is the conduit of the impersonal. In-decision shimmers at the cusp of the one-many, living it out in the multiplicity of the both-and. Being of relation.

Impersonal affects circulate, bending any notion of rectitude. "For the affect is not a personal feeling, nor is it a characteristic; it is the effectuation of a power of the pack that throws the self into upheaval and makes it reel" (Deleuze and Guattari 1987, 240). The pack: that field of forces, the minor sociality that experiments with how blackness makes a bodyworld. "Personhood has changed address – no longer embodied in the human corporeal entity, but in diffractive enlistments spread out in the environment" (Akomolafe 2021a, np). "[F]igures who nevertheless come to haunt Man as the bearers of an ontological dissonance, an immanent declension, we might call blackness" (Bradley and Ferreira da Silva 2021, np).

In the opacity of a poet(h)ics of relation,[18] blackness operates the turn that pulses the impersonal from identity. Its disruption unsettles. "The total exposure of blackness both enables and extin-

18 See Édouard Glissant, *Poetics of Relation* (Ann Arbor: University of Michigan Press, 1997); Denise Ferreira da Silva, "Toward a Black Poethics: The Quest(ion) of Blackness Toward the End of the World," *The Black Scholar* 44, no. 2 (2014): 81-97.

guishes the force of the modern ethical program, insofar as the disruptive capacity of blackness is a quest(ion) toward the end of the world. Blackness is a threat to sense, a radical questioning of what comes to be brought under the (terms of the) 'common'" (Bradley and Ferreira da Silva 2021, np). In the "threat to sense," there is more than one and less than many. In an ethics of the undercommon feel,[19] what stands out as given is not a figure but the consent not to be a single being. But be careful: the consent is not ours to give or take. The consent is in and of the world giving itself.

The earth gives existence opaquely, its field of relation pulsing us into the uneasy vacillation of activity and valuation. Akomolafe calls this "decolonial abundance." "Whatever you do, don't try to make the world a better place; instead, consider that the world might be trying to make you a better place" (Akomolafe 2021a, np).

The world is not ours to make. The world is the body affected and affecting. It is the force-flow of all that briefly resounds in the one of the many and the many of the one. Minor sociality is its grammar, its lexicon. To listen to it is to incline.

---

19 See Stefano Harney and Fred Moten, *The Undercommons: Fugitive Planning and Black Study* (Minor Compositions, 2013).

To hear it is to angle toward blackness.

"When there is nothing to govern, nothing to secure, there is blackness" (Harney and Moten 2021, 84).

The Untimely Impersonal

Neurodiverse time expresses itself in the minor sociality of the unparsable, time out of time, time devoid of executive function, time not only nonlinear but fundamentally ungraspable as a line or a block.

The unparsable is incalculable, outside the count. Its topology of spread a continuous array of folds, an exuberance of yield, the incalculable is not empty. It is one-many, singular-plural, all-at-once.

Neurodiverse time is out of the grasp of me and mine. It is not the expression of a person, but the feel of a worlding. In and of the world, in the catch of an act, in the array of all that moves between, neurodiverse time fields existence, and is fielded by it. There are of course handholds, momentary catchings that catch a subtraction in the making, but this finality of form is felt chiefly in the adjacency of what moves through it. An object may carry it, a thought, an action. But this carrying does not toe the line. It resonates across the field of experience. Time is felt in the overlap.

The impersonal is not exactly the opposite of the personal. If the personal is the movement through which a framing onto identity takes place, organizing existence into a form, parsing objects and subjects in order to create a standing-out of human existence, the impersonal is the force of all that moves relationally across that posture. The impersonal, like the transindividual in Gilbert Simondon, is the reminder that before it persons, and between the personings, and in excess of the person, there is an associated milieu, a fielding of tendencies, inflections, perspectives (1995).

If we begin with identity, with fixed form, if we assume a subject in advance of the world, any notion of existence is culled through the separation of body and world, object and subject, culture and nature. To begin with "person" is to extrude time from existence to feed it back in.

The present is the most contracted element of lived experience. Impersonality recognizes its speciousness (James 1890). The sense of present's nowness is due to a release into the world of a certain framing. We place ourselves in coincidence with activity's subtraction. There remains a shimmer, however. Presentness cleaves even as it carries future-pastness. The form-taking of presentness peaks as it leaves a shape behind, a shape already humming with the force of its reorienting by orientations as yet unparsed. What peaks to take the form of the present is a tweak in the density of existence unparsed.

The density of existence carries the dilation of what is already fading from it. Without presentness, there are no convergences, and convergences matter. Pure flow is unsustainable. The present is how experience stakes its mattering, exposing the density of a matter segregating itself from the force-of-form that propulsed it toward shape. The present materializes experience at the cusp where it is both retreating and beckoning, future-past co-composing. Neurodiverse time catches presentness forming but refuses to reduce existence to the shape it takes. This is not a willful refusal, as though there were a person on the outside refusing a shape already given. It is a refusal in the *agencement* of perception itself.

Qualitative differentials animate the density that is the dance of contraction-dilation. Inheritances are vital. The world does not emerge from a vacuousness – it is fed-forward by all that quivers at its edges. Neurodiverse time fields these tendencies in the thickness of overlaps that carry resonances across a bodying that is always also a worlding. To live is to cusp bodyworld in each activity, it is to be made by a world in-forming.

Neurodiverse time feels the force of extension as part of its own immanent shaping. The pulsing into activity of the world is directly felt, its bounce, its exuberance: the shape of enthusiasm.[20]

Neurotypical modalities of existence rely on form as block of existence. Their mode is always separation: body in world. This is taught from the earliest age. To hold this up requires a complex gymnastics. First, actuality and potentiality have to be reversed. What is there has to be conceived as given, and the person has to move into the world ahead of it. I is the protagonist of worlds always in retreat. Potential is negated in lieu of existing, quantifiable forms. Common-sense over associated milieu.

Neurodiverse time does not register in this account of time-parsed. The untimeliness of its worldings are not legible in the one-after-the-other time of existence cut to measure. In

---

20 For more on autistic perception and its attunement to the excess on form that shapes experience, see "The Shape of Enthusiasm" in Erin Manning, *Always More Than One: Individuation's Dance* (Durham: Duke University Press, 2013), 184-203.

an ethos of the pragmatics of the useless, the untimely impersonal catches life in the making, and makes itself through it. It feels and fields in a relational milieu eternally unsettled, spacetiming itself into existence in the density of what immanently unfolds. In doing so, it threatens all that is held by neurotypicality, all that is classified, organized.

Neurotypicality has no sociality. Its depleted mode of encounter produces no excess on itself, no reverberation, no resonance. Everything in its place, organized, metered. Networking is its mantra. Frontality defines this march toward the goal, face to face, eye to eye. Firm handshakes round it off, as we leapfrog over each other to our destination.

Mostly, neurotypicality is a backgrounded phenomenon. There is no reason to notice its workings because they work for us, they get us where we want to go, those of us who benefit from it. That it is an impoverished modality of existence is only discernible in the strange emptiness of our existences, as we sit back in our mortgaged properties, wondering what else we can own. Colonization has a long reach, its benefits reaped in the name of expediency long after we've already settled the land. No time to waste!

The untimely impersonal trembles at that threshold where worlds are still in flux and life remains unsettled. Attempts to consolidate tend to be failures. What is a product anyway when everything is still in movement? Where is I in the mix? Time is crafted in the interstices, taking "me" into the upheaval of worlds still forming. In the relational milieu, a sociality is germinating. This sociality does not presuppose the human. Usually there are more gripping encounters to be had. No interpersonality. No face to face. In the associated milieu of a field resonant with qualities – tonality edging into colour, affordance tuning toward form – a jostling of contrasts sidle each other. I is a sidling.

The minor sociality of tendencies sidling is born of processes. To make a day is to find the day, the density it has, the conviviality it makes. It is to practice a dramaturgy of edgings into existence that do not guarantee secure footing. It is to not know in advance if there will be a shape to align with, to live in immanent attunement to the relational fields that texture existence.

Minor sociality is never about exchange, interchange. It is not about me and you. Minor sociality retreats in the face of neurotypicality/whiteness and all it values. Minor sociality is the expression of worlds coming into themselves and the practice of composing this calls forth.

For each coming-into-itself of existence, there is a historical route. This historical route inflects the present, imbuing it with a quality of pastness reinvigorated. This inflection cannot be reduced to content, however. A historical route is not a state. It's a movement. The inflection carries the impersonality of what always exceeds the content in the flow from past to present.

In the coming into itself of a present, a good edge of potential actualizes, but there always remains an excess. Extension is not ultimately containable. This is why Whitehead calls it an "extensive continuum" (1978). Extension is a "relational complex" – a field that carries inflections already affected by the futurity they call forth in their coming-to-be (1978, 66).

To directly perceive the schizz of time bending into relational complex is the exquisite beauty of neurodiversity. To live the metastability of existence so completely is also to be continuously unmoored.

Much is said about repetition, replay, in relation to neurodiversity, often pejoratively. So much is missed in this critique. Neurodiverse replay has nothing to do with fixed horizons.

Quite the contrary, the perseveration of a taste of life returned to again and again has to do with the necessity of momentarily stabilizing the vertigo of an unceasingly shifting landscape. The untimely impersonal pulses between the rhythm of existence slightly dampened by repetition and the unwieldy excess of all that colours itself into existence, the pulse of life-living felt in the vicissitudes of all edgings in and out of the world's force-of-form. To be always and only in the midst requires a lived attunement to how the worlding times itself into bodying, in all of its incorporeal materiality.

To feel the force of time in the making is to field the world from the perspective of the relational complex itself. There is no longer any I at the center of experience. It is the relational matrix that underlies experience in "indefinite divisibility" and "unbounded extension" (Whitehead 1978, 66).

Indefinite divisibility is akin to impersonal density. Divisibility happens in every present passing, but it must not be confounded with the continuum. That is to say, when division happens, what occurs is a densification of an angle on experience now actualized. Spacetime is made in that actualization, the continuum oriented toward matter. But unbounded extension is never fully captured by what forms – it is shape without form, which is to say, shapeability.

Shapeability is sidled sensuously in neurodiverse time. This is not a metaphorical sidling. The world in formation is felt, lived, in direct perception, sideways. This feels like tonalities, affordances, qualities. It feels like affect coursing through an extended bodyworld. What it never feels like is a thing.

Density of experience is only ever relational. Minor sociality cleaves this relationality not by forcing it into form but by creating openings for it. The impersonal flows through this untethered force of existence, making us again and again.

This making turns around a standpoint. "[The] extensive continuum expresses the solidarity of all possible standpoints throughout the whole process of the world" (Whitehead 1978, 66) Standpoints of the extensive continuum are inflections in solidarity with the movement of existence itself. "[The extensive continuum] is not a fact prior to the world; it is the first determination of order – that is, of real potentiality – arising out of the general character of the world" (66). The stand is not a measure, not a form. It is a tendency, an opening onto itself of existence inflected. "In its full generality beyond the present epoch, it does not involve shapes, dimensions, or measurability; these are additional determinations of real potentiality arising from our cosmic epoch" (66). Standpoints cast to the foreground the conditions of the cosmic epoch while being made by them.

The standpoint carries impersonality with it. In the subtraction from the welter, in the selecting-out of an angle on existence, a mode of existence comes into itself. This mode carries a certain tonality, a qualitative edge, that differentiates it from other modes. It is unique in its way of carrying potential, and manifesting stability. The impersonality that runs through is also unique. Neurodiverse time attunes to this uniqueness. This unique quality of expression running through the standpoint *is the world.* Existence is nothing else than the relational milieu it is made of. Existence is its formation – force-of-form.

The contract upheld by major accounts of spacetime is clear. We know it as colonization, imperialism, racism, ableism. To fit is to fit into the form prescribed. To count is to be parsable for the count. To exist is to be part of a world.

The problem is: to uphold the world as outside our-selves is to have to constantly reduce it to simple location. It is to police the movements of bodying. It is to regulate difference. Systems must be kept in check. Variations must be muted. And all that resists capture must be cast out.

Major accounts of spacetime engender the continued settling of existence. Settler colonialism is an ongoing process, its afterlife felt in all the ways bodies are cordoned off, identified, gridded, organized, racialized. The extensive continuum does not involve shapes, dimensions, or measurability. These are aftereffects of process, process backgridded into form. In order to justify its violence, settler colonialism must develop a concept of spacetime that mutes *a* nature, that disavows the emergent quality of perspectives making worlds. It must reduce life to deadening binaries, it must keep land "out there." To justify the clearing, it must reduce any account of life to marketing, to capital. It must reify modes of knowing that privilege those networks that count, that can be counted. It must believe in humanism above all, and be willing to go to war for it. All of this despite the feel, the field, of what the extensive continuum generates at the cusp of its occasioning, as it shifts back into the potential of the relational complex.

The untimely impersonal shifts the tense from the I am toward the it is. It is a shimmer, it is a field, it is a vertiginously empty-full hole, it is an uneasy untimeliness. It is, it is.

Uneasy untimelinesses are concrescences, shapings into existence of worlds in the forming. That they peak into their own singular density is important but only ever part of the story. Experience is rife with all that still courses through it, inheritances and pulls toward unknowability alike. I loses its footing: experience is the coming into itself of a concrescence that cannot but exceed the I we thought we were. For while the concrescence of existence produces "a regional standpoint in the world," a certain density that conjoins the me we are becoming, limiting the field of potentiality, the "solidarity of one world" also courses through it, that oneness of time that enfolds while it extends, contracting-dilating (Whitehead 1978, 67).

The oneness of time doesn't mean that time is homogenous. It simply means that time cannot be neatly subdivided: each expression of time produces new pathways for experience that in turn activate new modes of living. Every account of experience carries the oneness of the world with it, not as the wholeness of one, but as the angle on it of a perspective it carries. There is no perspective *on* the world. Perspective is *in* the world, *of* the relational complex. This "epochal theory of time" refuses any externality, any colonial objectiveness. To be in the world is to be in time, and to be in time is to make the world, one-many. “The many become one, and are increased by one” (Whitehead 1978, 21).

At the cusp where experience and density coalesce to shape existence into its texture of presentness, what is produced is indisputable. It exists. The untimely impersonal is not a negation of the shape experience takes. It sidles all processes of shaping, even while it fields their excess, living at the interstices of form and force.

Techniques are necessary. Without them, the cacophonous excess of life-living in all its intensity is overwhelming. Often this continual vividness of experience teeming results in a kind of standstill, a vibratory inertia, the tremor of the too-muchness of existence so dense that there is no way to directly compose with it, to be composed by it. This produces a deactivated bodying, a modality that decouples with any sense of space or time. A pure body-continuum. When the force-of-form is too intense, techniques must be invented to navigate the welter. Because to remain in the edges and curves and echoes of experience forming all the time is impossible: a body needs to contract.

The many and the one, in overlap. Multiplicity

layers, surfacing existence topologically. How to compose with an "apportioning without dividing," Gilles Deleuze asks, citing Bergson (1991, 80)? How to be "one and several" without splitting, cutting, counting (80)?

Refuse the binary between the divisible and the indivisible. Recognize the affordance a ritual provides and follow its lure. Dwell in the structure of a repetition until you can hear its rhythm. Feel the cadence of a shaping and move into it. Explore the simultaneity of fluxes and how they "occupy the same duration, [holding] each other in the duration of a third" (Deleuze 1991, 81).

The third is not a person. It is the activity of impersonally apportioning, of being apportioned by the event: "there will now only be impersonal time in which all things will flow" (Bergson 1922, 47, *translation modified*).

The time of the impersonal is one time, one-many, always more than one. This is what neurodiverse time fields, and what it feels. Time is a texture that bends and shapes worlds in the making. The relational complex produced in the bending is an aesthetic sociality, and it must be said to be black, if black life is the condition of minor sociality in the approximation of proximity of neurodiversity and black life.

The Speculative Garden

Descartes had to call in God, in order to push his bodies around.
—Alfred North Whitehead

Whatever you do, don't try to make the world a better place; instead, consider that the world might be trying to make you a better place.
—Bayo Akomolafe

Part 1

Scene 1

The trees are a concern. We invite him in to cull. The solar panels are shaded by the tallest ones. Decisions have to be made. We can't cut them all down. How much energy is enough?

Sustainable: capable of being endured; continuing to exist.[21]

The solar panels are really in the wrong place. More money should go into raising them, into pushing them above the tree tops. Strange, this stand-off with the forest, caught up with the desire to reduce the burning of fossil fuels, to not need the generator on those cloudy days where the sun just can't get through.

He comes and we stand on the edge of the cliff and look out at the river. Which trees should fall? He points at trees. We nod. Or change our mind. No, not that birch, it's so beautiful. There is no rational standpoint. A bit of shade brought on by this one is not so bad, is it? But that one, yes, that one should go. Down with the conifers!

I go down to where he is. He doesn't talk much. Instead, he holds his hands in front of his eyes, mimicking taking a photograph. Yes, he says.

There's a path here, I say. Can we move the fallen trees off the path? I love the moss. He looks down. Yes, he says, we will make sure the path remains. The dog runs around us, excited by the sound of the chainsaw.

---

21 *Oxford English Dictionary,* 2nd edition (1989), s.v. "sustainable."

Scene 2

We are disappointed. The sun is still not coming up high enough in the sky. November in the north is hard for solar sites. We would have to cut down all the trees – or at least their tips – to benefit from its weak glare. He is still cutting, moving, sorting. Every once in a while I see him stand, look around, his photographic gaze scanning the surround. Sometimes he tells me something he sees. He is hard to understand. Some people tell me there is a story there. I think it's neurodiversity. He feels the forest, and for that there are no words.

Now he is cutting the downed trees into logs. Since we purchased the land, wood has been our most constant companion. Has there been a day when we haven't cut/split/carried/stacked/burned wood?

The sun remains low. We return to the edge of that small cliff often, willing the sun to be higher.

Scene 3

What does he see? What is the seeing-feeling of a forest, in a forest? I accompany him to the old-growth maple forest, where a number of trees have fallen on the sap-line. The ease of flow the sap lines facilitate is inversely proportional to the work it takes to keep them up in the wake of fallen trees. I have purchased a small chainsaw, but the truth is, I can't see the forest.

I walk behind him and listen to his quiet monologue, his language, as always, mostly unintelligible. I see him scanning, holding his camera-hands in front of his eyes, catching the field in the frame. He says something about the beech. Did I understand correctly that its acidity is bad for the maple? We continue walking up the hill, checking each line as we cross it. Yes, he says, pointing at a large tree. That one needs to be down. See, it's unhealthy. It will fall in a year. Look, this one can't thrive. Yup, down.

The dog runs in circles, sometimes returning to us with a branch.

Whenever he spots a tree angling to fall on the line, he stops. He looks for gravitational angles, wonders about the direction of the wind. He knows how to topple the tree so it falls where it needs. He also knows when he should leave it alone.

Scene 4

The lumberjacks in northern Quebec live in a subsistence economy that is largely extractive. And yet, theirs is an attunement much more refined than mine when it comes to what needs to be left standing and what is in the way of the forest's ability to thrive.

The mirror-hands see both. They see-feel what is in the way and what is lively with potential. Despite all the cutting they've done, they know how to recognize a healthy environment, and they are practiced in a respect for its majesty. Theirs is not a maudlin gaze. Sustainability is not their language. The forest is their sustenance. And yet it would be wrong to say that their approach is not ecological in its care for the surround. I wonder how to square the extractivist subsistence-stance with the sensitivity in the field-framing? How to avoid falling into a moralist all-or-nothing stance about some imagined notion of an untouched, pristine environment?

Scene 5

We hear talk of "going back to the land." It often comes up when we talk about the 3E land project.

What is this "going back?" What is this land that populates the outskirts, that lives in the beyond of the pavement?

We didn't go back to the land.[22] We entered the forest to better encounter the forest-of-the-pavement. Distantism reigns large in this strange inadequation of here and there. Distantism is the term John Lee Clark gives to the ableist ocularcentric account of how existence values itself (2017). Distantism is the presupposition that the world comes in the guise of establishing shots, ready at a distance for us to enter it. Distantism is the value we put on all that is already in place, our bodies the agents of those acts that diagonalize it, space left intact in the crossing, body left standing, a perpendicular assemblage out of feel.

With his hands in front of his eyes, the forest-field in the frame, it might be tempting to posit a quality of distantism. Is that what he's after, scanning the forest for what needs to be culled? I don't think so. The gesture, it seems to me, is relational before it is establishing. And in any case the body never remains upright – it leans, keels, crouches. The aim is not to single out so

22 "Put aside visions of 'back to the land,' and just think land – some of it is wild, some of it is urban, a lot of it is ecologically devastated" (Simpson 2017, 195).

much as to amplify, to see-feel the abundance in the body-world overlap. The vista is attuned to not at a spatial distance. It is felt in the weave of its tangled surround.

Distantism has disdain for the tangle. Its stakes are colonial: divide and conquer. In the overview, there is no heterogeneity, there is nothing to tend to. Cut it down. Clear it. Make way.

Interlude

Distantism frames existence without the hands-on-face. Clark recognizes it in the figure of the intervenor in DeafBlind culture. What is this mediator for, this intervenor, who facilitates access for the DeafBlind? He is the navigator of distances. She tells you, before you even knew to ask, what there is to see-hear, at a distance. Her aim will not be to influence you, but to give it to you "like it is." Leaving you without bearings, she is your distantist hold on the world, giving you the world in drips and drabs. You will come to feel this is all the world is, this distance. He means well, but truly, he is the representative of the most depleted account of existence: its logistics. Because remember: her role is to stay objective, to stand aside while holding you up, steering you through, keeping you away from the thick of feel. Because even with the best intentions, the world he moves you through is one which dreads your unwieldy metatactile feel, a world neurotypical in its systemic organization of what counts as body, as knowledge. The intervenor, in the neurotypical belief that walking stiffly across space, body unmoored, will secure the most direct access to existence, will do so in the absence of any handholds. Out of feel, your world will be reduced to this impoverished schema of coordinates peppered with ocularcentric accounts of what will remain out of reach.

Distantism is mediation. It lives and profits from the belief that there is no world which is not already accounted for. And it tells its story plainly: propriety requires us to move through the world without too much rub. Body-world cleave.

Part 2

Scene 1

The gesture again: hands-on-face, the forest pulled right in, its tangle felt. He smiles. Yes, he says.

This speculative gesture carries an appetite to see-feel the forest differently. In the act of framing, an in-gathering of the field occurs. This in-gathering, a backgroundingforegrounding, produces a selection. This selection is active: the hand-frame is not meant to stabilize. It is meant to angle into the forest's singular quality. A movement-effect is sought in the selecting-out. What is oriented toward is the relational field of that particular angle.

In the forest, one selected vista looks a lot like another to the untrained encounter. What the selecting-out in the framing gesture does is to allow a certain parsing of what is actually an extremely varied environment. What to an unintuitive forest body seems relatively static is vertiginous with micromovements. The gesture is not a taming one, but an inducing one. To see-feel the movements is to attune to what can be culled from the field.

Alfred North Whitehead strangely calls this activity of culling-for-intensity *reason*. The function of reason, he writes, is "to promote the art of life" (1958, 4). Reason has always felt like exactly the wrong concept for this activity of subtraction that accentuates existence. Sometimes he calls its most creative edge the "appetition of appetitions" (33). Speculative reason has the quality of an *agencement*, an in-gathering of what out-gathers. Emergent valuation?

Emergent valuation – the force of reason at its most speculative edge – does its culling in an ethos of a pragmatics of the useless, which is to say, it co-composes in a surround to produce a quality of vitality, a mode of existence as of yet untethered to the modalities of use of existence-foretold.

Emergent valuation: that quality that unmoors the expected, producing conditions for value. Reason unreasoned in appetite for what stirs, and reorients.

Scene 2

Emergent valuation cusps existence. It is the force of a cleave that reorients, tipping expectations. In the forest, two tendencies are continuously at work. One is toward degradation, decay. The other is toward exultance. The first tendency is pragmatic, the second speculative. The speculative pragmatism of this tensile weave is its force – one needs the other. What is being gestured toward in the framing is nothing so simple as the death-life binary. A quality of existence is being attuned to that exceeds any simple notion of decay versus growth, or any notion that decay isn't also a complex process. At both limits, the world is undergoing change, and its process is replete with potential.

Sustainability is always the wrong term for this excess on itself of life-living. This is not about the common denominator of endurance, of almost-not-better-than-the-baseline modes of living. What is felt-seen in the framing is how the forest exceeds expectations; how it exuberantly defies them.

What is the art of life? Must the value of life be limited to longevity? Where does the artfulness of existence express itself? For Whitehead, any notion of "the survival of the fittest" must be understood to be a fallacy (1958, 4). The art of life is not reducible to what endures. To live long is not necessarily to live well: "the art of life is *first* to be alive, *secondly* to be alive in a satisfactory way, and *thirdly* to acquire an increase in satisfaction. It is at this point of our argument that we have to recur to the function of Reason, namely the promotion of the art of life" (1958, 8). The art of life is more than longevity – it is enjoyment, excess-on-itself, speculative force. "In fact life itself is comparatively deficient in survival value. The art of persistence is to be dead" (4).

In the forest, survival is certainly at work, in all its majestic endurance. There are enormous rock formations, no doubt the remnants of a glacier's passage. These rocks, the largest I have seen in Quebec, are covered in moss and small bushes, lively with insects. Downed trees are habitat for amphibians, their trunks sometimes as wide as a meter around. The trees are remarkably old for a Quebec forest – very tall, gnarly, the branches opening up only at their tips, odd for maple trees as I know them from elsewhere. The art of persistence is very much in view. But in the tangle, something else is at work – a relational web constantly in flux is nourishing the field. Even more: it is producing it.

How things thrive is not strictly mappable onto the useful.

Holding his hands to his face, in the relation, speculatively attuned, the hands act less as blockers than as amplifiers. This is not primarily about vision, though vision does play a role. His attuning is closer to what Tina Campt calls "frequency," an attunement to what amplifies the nature of experience, to what is felt, haptically, in and of the surround. In the attunement to all that is here-now, he catches a becoming-frequency (2021, 127).

Scene 3

The art of life is the capacity for difference. It is the modality, in the field, for life to exceed the form it seems to take. It is the way the more-than of the trees, of the rocks, forests, come into the feel, exposing all that weaves through them. To cut, to clear, in the ethos of the tangle, cannot be simplified into the concept of extraction. To cut under these conditions is not to clear out, it is to clear in. It is to amplify, in the sonic surround, the capacity for the environment to thrive. It is to see-feel its verve.

Emergent valuation refuses the omnipotent stance of the surveyor. Whitehead calls it "the speculative reason," to emphasize the difference between the reduction that leads to the deadening aspect of endurance as ultimate value of survivability and the quality of the more-than that produces a "conceptual flash," that tunes existence toward the appetition of appetitions (1958, 23). The speculative reason emergently values, enthusiastically refusing the limitations of all we have come to expect. The speculative reason moves us in an abeyance of our-selves. Life-living becomes us.

Anarchy is at work in this "counter-agency," "counter" in the sense that its agency is closer to an *agencement*, to an in-gathering of tendency that potentializes more than it realizes (Whitehead 1958, 25). The aim here is not to come to ultimate form, to stabilize. The aim is to aim, to be in process, and in process, to entangle further into the relations that allow that quality of tipping that keeps life on its toes, in its art.

Scene 4

In a philosophy of pure feeling,[23] feeling is what propulses experience. Feeling is not Personal – it is not "mine." Feeling is the momentum of life's artfulness. Feeling motors existence into quality (Whitehead 1978, 87-88).

This process-philosophical orientation refuses reason as the moderator, the mediator, of existence-culled. Reason-become-valuation is feeling-tone. This vibratory quality is not in excess of form: form is but an angle of its activity – the force-of-form. What we distantly see is never its pulse. To see-feel it, new qualities of encounter have to be practiced. Knees on rock, nose to moss, the forest is (of) us.

23 Alfred North Whitehead describes process philosophy as a "philosophy of pure feeling," as opposed to a Kantian "philosophy of pure reason" (1978, 113).

Distantism has kept us in the belief that to be here is to be "back" to the land.

We have always been here, in the midst.

Scene 5

Anarchy troubles the vista. What is seen-felt is not reducible to the frame. Indeed, the frame was never a frame, really. It was an action much like covering your ears to hear better, or closing your eyes to see better. Techniques for attuning have to be honed.

Process's emergent valuation requires techniques. It must remain "untrammeled by method" (Whitehead 1958, 61). Techniques are practices. In the gesture of culling-for-intensity there is no one way. Each surround has its quality of movement, its angle on existence. The pathway must be drawn every time anew. Without respect for the anarchy of all that exceeds the form things take, there is only extraction. In the pull of speculative reason's techniques of framing, in the neurodiverse see-feel that queers dominant neurotypical extractivist models of ableist existence, the chainsaw increasingly works as a nimble instrument that amplifies complexity rather than as a blunt tool of destruction. For it must be said: neurodiversity is not reducible to a person, it is a way, a modality that endangers the systemic hierarchy of all that neurotypicality values, which is to say, whiteness, colonialism, ableism.

As we walk together, climbing over fallen trees, I am led to another way of being in the forest, a way that speaks as much to the space of the surround as to its time.

In the anarchic force of valuation, what is drawn by the cut is also a timeline. To cull is to open up the forest to the exposure of more than one time signature, to more than one rhythm. This is not a question of scale but of metastability: different rhythms of existence in co-composition. The forest spirals spacetime in its living-forth.

We don't speak of any of this as we sweat our way up. I am still following, watching closely which tree is cleared, which logs are piled for later retrieval, and which ones are encouraged to remain on the ground to foster new habitat. We don't have a philosophical language that binds us, or even an ecological one. I don't know how to speak of how important it is to me that this old-growth forest continues to thrive. But I do know that his touch is gentle, and that there is, in each movement forward, in each reacquainting gesture of framing the surround, a care for all that lives, artfully.

Part 3

Scene 1

The long winter colours existence in a play of light and shadow. The shades of light and dark in the layers of snow and ice, a slight tinge of blue-green, a reflection of the often starkly sunny skies, bright in the minus thirty degree weather, the contrasting greens of the evergreens, the quality of bark, dark brown and grey and green – these colour the field. With the crisp and often excruciatingly cold air comes a certain tonality, a play of density, light become volumetric, not a monotone so much as a subdued rhythm, a low frequency, intense in its movement.

Colour is movement, imbuing more than painting the surround.

With the burst of spring growth, a new angle of colour's feeling-tone permeates the landscape, its vividness as olfactory as it is visual. Thick mud, the remnant of more than a meter of snow, sinks us into the humus of the forest regenerating. Wildflowers will soon take over, a surprise, always, in their persistent impatience to populate the post-winter barrenness. Paul Cézanne writes of "coloring sensations" that "give light" (1978, 123).[24] Josef Albers speaks of "colour action," of the feeling of "colour relatedness" (1963, 1). That colour is movement is a reminder that it is fielded in an excess of vision, in an opacity of relatedness, an action that can never be situated in the distantism of a body-world separation. Colour is relational movement, not object. Colour is lived abstraction, speculative actant in a field as yet undetermined, movement of forces in tenuous contact. When asked how he produces this vibrant matter, Cézanne replies that it is nature that gives us the means of achieving it (1978, 123).

Colour is plane of existence, feeling-tone tuned toward a frequency that is not reducible to pigment – to red or blue or green. Colour cannot be seen in separation. To see-feel colour is to be in the frequency of its adjacency. Cézanne speaks of "fusioning," of "prismatic heat." "Only volumes matter. Air between objects to paint well. Like sensation between thoughts to think well" (1978, 124).

The world colouring itself is the speculative at work, the affective interplay of the relational tangle. This feeling-tone is met affectively. Spring comes with the feel of all that flows between, the

---

24 My translations throughout.

flowering-effect irreducible to any one plant. In the art of living well, the world's colouring beckons vistas that foster new modes of bodying. Not sustainability: transversality.[25]

Scene 2

The three ecologies in overlap: the social, the conceptual and the environmental. Not 1+1+1 but the production of subjectivity entangled, across all planes of existence. Speculative reason pulses this production into act, parsing the field into its acuteness, fielding a foregrounding of what stands out. Another way of saying this: we are made in the interstices of the overlap, subjectivity produced environmentally in us, through us. Any category of human is a distantist dream, a dream that kills (life).[26] Ecology is this thirdness,

25 "Being in the company of those people made me reflect on the myth of sustainability, invented by corporations to justify their theft of our idea of nature" (Krenak 2020, 20).

26 Indigenous writer and movement leader Ailton Krenak, of the Krenak peoples, writes: "In 2018, on the cusp of being assailed by a new political establishment in Brazil, people asked me: 'What are the Indians going to do in the face of all this?' I said: 'The Indians have been holding out for over five hundred years now. I'm more worried about the whites, and what they're going to

this in-and-beyond quality of an us-ness that is always in deference of it-self. We are coloured in this fielding, "we" the force of all that exceeds us, of all that is born of an excursion up the mountain, in the culling-for-verve. Speculative reason makes us: we are its emergent valuation, we, nature.

In moving colour, there is only relational movement, its anarchic edge a taunt to any commitment to the representation of the useful. The art of life is a drive toward amplification, toward excess, in an ethos of a pragmatics of the useless.

The temptation, in the distantist clear, is to make it useful in that particular way that moralizes the earth and our "return" to it. Make it edible. Make yourself independent. Call yourself a survivalist.

But there is no independence in this vista of the tangled surround. The feeling-tone of existence transversalizing is relational through and through.

Nature: "anything encountered by creative procedure which may be procedurally construed as having been already in operation" (Massumi 2019, 12). To be in operation: activist philosophy. "Ultimately, the thinking of speculative pragmatism that is activist philosophy belongs to nature. Its aesthetico-politics compose a nature philosophy.

---

do to get out of this one'" (2020, 35-36).

The occurrent arts in which it exhibits itself are politics of nature" (Massumi 2011, 28).

Nature as occurrent art: aesthesis, sensation in the fold, feeling-felt, in abeyance of the me standing out. "In activist philosophy *to be is to be felt*" (Massumi 2011, 20).

Scene 3

Emergent valuation at its speculative limit – the feeling-tone of existence, in moving colour – is the naturing of relation, relation's nature.

Relation's nature is univocal. Its power is that it cannot be separated out, that there is no separation between what it is and how it acts. There are no parts to nature, no aggregates. "The order of nature is single and unique, it is everywhere a single power to act; being affirms itself in a single sense for the multitude of modes that differ infinitely. The unity of the substantial being is not ultimately a unifying unit. Rather, it comes in the univocity of potential, which is expressed in as many gradations as there are modes" (Combes 2020, 152).

Leaning on Spinoza while gesturing toward Simondon, Muriel Combes amplifies the carrying quality of nature's univocity, its preindividual force. The preindividual does not precede an individual. It is the quality of existence that transduces individuation at all levels.

Scene 4

He pauses, catching his breath as we scramble over the logs, still on our way up, lifting dead branches off the sap line, liberating it from debris. He looks around, wipes his forehead, takes out a cigarette. The dog runs around us, trying to lure us into a game. But we are too tired to throw the stick, so we sit for a bit. He points at a mushroom, points to some chaga on the birch. I can't quite see it. We talk about all the ways it can be used as medicine, as infusion. Make coffee with it, he says, and laughs. Or at least, that's what I think he says. I look again, trying to spot it.

His hands on his face he scans again, this time looking down, toward the maple shack. Now he is looking at the mountain from a different angle, seeing-feeling its gravitational lines from the top, noting where the sap lines converge. He points to an old maple, showing me the infestation of ants and the signs of the woodpecker. The tree's weakness is being exploited. We won't take it down yet – it will produce sap for a few years still. But then it will have to come down or it will fall on the line.

What he sees-feels: the force of the preindividual at work, the way the preindividual sculpts time through its Tarkowskian rhythmic pressure (Deleuze 1989). For there is here a cinematic quality, what Kelann Currie-Williams might call an afterimage – "a type of lingering or persistence that stretches across vision and the auditory all at once" (2022).

This "sensual ensemble" is lived (Moten 2003, 189). More prehended than perceived, which is to say, activated in the grasp of becoming a perceptual force, the tangle of relation pulses into being in the very same gesture that the perceiver himself is forested. There is no clear-cut separation: being is becoming.

Nature natures. Processes are moved into activity through the force of the preindividual that courses through them. We become at this interstice, our human quality quivering in the sensual ensemble. The ensemble, in moving colour, is never a being. "An individuation does not succeed another" (Combes 2020, 155). It is not that there was a human perceiving and then a nature naturing. "When people speak of imagining a new possible world, it's in the sense of rearranging relations and spaces, introducing new understandings of what we recognize as nature, as if we were not nature ourselves" (Krenak 2020, 65). Nature is not a container. It is the carrying itself, the force that moves the preindividual across the tangle of relation. Any form it individuates is replete with the tangle of all that is still moving through it. We are made in the crease of the encounters its prehensions activate. We are not other to these encounters. We are born of the problem nature poses. "[I]f a new individuation can happen to the already individuated, it is according to a pre-individual part that it contains, and will function as a starting point for a newly arriving problem (*problématique*)" (Combes 2020, 155).

The problem motors existence. It is its speculative reason. That is to say, nature is the quality of a problem activating fields of thought. In the encounter's afterimage, nature's thinking is felt. This is what is seen-not-seen in the act of backgroundingforegrounding. It is not the forest so much that is caught here, but the preindividual of its pulsing composition, of our pulsing composition. Not one-two, but one-many, univocal.

Interlude

Nature's individuations are never reducible to the one-two, 1+1. It is not site, not state. "Nature... is that very capacity within the state of things that renders further individuations possible" (Combes 2020, 156). The operative problem of nature, its *problématique*, is the movement that moves it into naturing. Movement – in moving colour – is a threat to the status quo. It does violence to all claims of property. It cannot be owned.

"Misplaced concreteness" is the platform we rely on for the ongoing colonialism that settles us, those of us who reign, who stand-out from nature, who extract it to our benefit (Whitehead 1978, 7). Whiteness thrives in this "fallacy of misplaced concreteness" that "consists in neglecting the degree of abstraction involved when an actual entity is considered merely so far as it exemplifies certain categories of thought" (7-8). In the systemic whiteness that paints nature as site for extraction, as site for the taking (of pleasure, of wealth), thought is reduced to the most depleted representation of the useful. We take what is not there to give, and we keep taking it. "Corporate sustainability managers have become the sacerdotes of a new planetary order, self-righteously preaching something their employers, by their very nature, can't practice" (Krenak 2020, 21).

Part 4

In the midst, the problem beckons. The problem is the counter-agency, and the lure, the shimmer for all that moves life into the art of living. Nature is its speculative reason, not as state, but as conduit.

This conduit cannot be seen. It is not of the order of the visual, if the visual is understood to be singled out from the viscerality of sense. Nature is not distantist. It has no single vantage point, no preexisting perspective. "Any local agitation shakes the whole universe" (Whitehead 1968, 138).

Naturing nature is feeling-tone, transmuted not from form to form, but flow to flow. "There is no nature apart from transition" (Whitehead 1968, 152). Thick with preindividual force, nature is indiscernible as such, parsed momentarily in the hands of a framing, but in excess always, of any true capture.

This is not to say that nature evades all stabilizing tendencies. There are of course infinite repetitions in the course of the histories of growth and decay, but what stands out most emphatically is how it differs. This speculative edge is its anarchic share.

At its most abstract, on the speculative edge of how nature exceeds itself – how it *is* excess

– naturing nature reveals its capacity to differ. The speculative reason does its work here, its "appetition of appetitions" expressing nature's most ardent creativity (Whitehead 1958, 33). The appetition of appetitions is emergent valuation at its most exuberant limit. In abeyance of the constraints of the pragmatic, existence bursts with speculative potential.

At this limit, "a factor of anarchy" is agitating (Whitehead 1958, 33). The anarchic pushes up against the expectation that nature stay in its place, that it be held in the form-taking of a site. There is no site in this anarchival pulse of life making itself. There are only relationscapes (Manning 2009). "Apart from anarchic appetition, nature is doomed to slow descent towards nothingness" (Whitehead 1958, 34).

Part 5

Permaculture, sometimes understood as "permanent agriculture," other times as "permanent culture," is premised on an attunement to the land, and to what it defines as nature's ways, the long arm of history always poised toward a past where the earth was not yet in need of regeneration. Its applications are sensible, and inventive, their modes of knowing most often legacies of centuries of lived Indigenous experiences. Its wager? Look at things from a different angle.[27] Catch an incline, and follow its flow. Find the orientation, and irrigate from there. Grow in companionship. Be interested in what blossoms. Make of it an edge. Give up on the hard line, on the fence. Plant sharing into the process. Let the liminal draw you in.

The 3E land project moves with many of permaculture's propositions. But a nagging problem presents itself through one of its main motors: scaling-up.

Nature's appetite is never toward scaling-up, if scaling-up is understood as a modality that fosters the growth of a system through replication so that the system can do its work across more than one constituency. Nature's urge is to differ in an ethos of speculative pragmatism. In its multiplication of conduits, its orientation is toward the emergent valuation of the tangle of relation in its local complexity. Its aim: how to thrive in interconnection. In a living refusal of any concept of survival of the fittest, nature's creativity fosters an infinity of overlapping times and spaces.

---

27 https://m.facebook.com/watch/?v=448988392893391&_rdr.

Nature's naturing is never a coherent whole. In this emergent collectivity of life-living there is no boundary. Scaling-up requires bounded processes. And it requires us to stand outside them.

In the forest, on the land, we must be wary of (trans)planting our-selves. Our gardens must remain speculative, their urge to vary stronger than our urge to grow them to scale. Because scale always means stability, and stability implies a reduction, a lessening of that art of life that reaches, infinitely, beyond its-self.

Sustainability has the whiff of decay. It feels like the lowest common denominator of a practice that has stopped naturing. In this holding pattern, a certain levelling is accomplished. A methodology is set in place so that processes can be streamlined. A necessary evil, we are told. We have always found ways to subtract our-selves from difference in the taming of nature.

It is tempting, in a time of ecological devastation, to look for solutions ("the problem is the solution"[28]) and to map these solutions onto processes that can scale. There is no doubt that the monocultures of the world (and of the mind,

---

28 "The problem is the solution" is a central tenet of permaculture. See Bill Mollison, *Permaculture: A Designer's Manual* (Sisters Creek: Tagari Publications, 1988).

as permaculture co-founder David Holmgren says[29]), are suffocating life. It makes sense to want to make an effort to make more legible the practices that have heretofore been limited to a few backyards, to a farm here and there. But is this need for legibility, this desire to map process onto usefulness, not part of the problem?[30] Do we really want to make sense at this juncture? Should we not be in the aesthesis instead, in the activist philosophy, in the exuberance of a sense too exalted to be common, in defiance of its distantist frame? Is the scaling-up not the death knell of the anarchic share that amplifies difference?

Twelve principles direct permaculture. Its ethos: care (for the planet, for people, for the system, in the guise of a return of the surplus to the people who most need it). At its best – a culture of abundance. The principles that direct the ethos are lived in an attunement to what is already underway. Begin by engaging, in a posture of curiosity. Orient to where and how energy is available, or depleted. Be aware of passive ways

29 https://holmgren.com.au/writing/the-problem-is-the-solution-but-solutions-can-turn-back-into-the-same-old-problems/.

30 https://holmgren.com.au/writing/the-problem-is-the-solution-but-solutions-can-turn-back-into-the-same-old-problems/.

of amplifying energetic resources. Be aware that problems can be solutions (and that solutions can be problems). Commit to renewables and produce no waste. Attune to patterns and integrate wherever possible. Be curious about slower, smaller solutions. Be interested in diversity. Value the edge. Be nimble in the face of change.[31]

The lure to scale lives as the dark edge of those slower, smaller solutions, of those ethical guidelines that celebrate the nimble qualities of experimentation. The problem is: to scale is not only to grow bigger. To scale is to shift modalities, to import methodological concerns into a process from outside its organic orientation, to impose onto it a value system that more concertedly coincides with an existing account of how existence is valued.

Despite these very real dangers, and the awareness of their limitations within permaculture circles, the temptation to bring the process into the mainstream remains strong, the aim of course to shift the ways of monocultural agriculture and our dependence on fossil fuels. This attention to scale can be heard in almost any gathering of the founders of permaculture, invited to speak about its future, and the future of the planet. An

---

31 https://earth.fm/blog/permaculture-principles/.

example of this is a 2022 "bioneers" discussion on scaling permaculture moderated by Penny Livingston.[32] The Earth is "out of control," Livingston begins. We must use permaculture tools to "turn the Earthship around," moving from "environmental degradation" toward "ecological regeneration." "We got this," she says. "The problems are increasingly complex but the solutions are embarrassingly simple." The question is, "do we have the political, economical will to do this."

On the panel, Maddy Harland, David Holmgren, and Mark Shepard share their thoughts on "scaling-up." Holmgren begins with hesitation. Scale is a concern in his approach, but he remains more ambivalent than the others. His operating mantra remains "to change the world one household at a time," it seems, but less for the reasons I suggest above than due to the fact that he has seen very little evidence that scaling-up works. "Small and slow solutions can stimulate and leverage larger scale change," he says. Livingston responds to his talk of different scenarios (in the ocean, in suburbs, in the forest), disregarding his ambivalence: "those are all incredible solutions that can be applied at scale. Just to illustrate that we can do this." When it's her turn, Maddy Harland speaks

32 https://www.youtube.com/watch?v=DNrLqdNQNBE.

about community school gardens, scaling-up by moving the knowledge of permaculture into the curriculum. "It has to be about awakening people to the possibilities, to seeing things as systems and not just disparate entities, to thinking long-term." She emphasizes the necessity of fair share as future care, planting for the generations to come. Mark Shepard interprets permanent agriculture as farming working with the ethos of small, slow change, regenerating land "using nature's playbook." As with the other speakers, Shepard returns to an image of pre-colonization, a time before fossil fuels, before land degradation. "If we are going to feed ten billion people," he says, discussing "processing product at scale," "and manage economically on our small holdings, we need to work collectively." Only then can we "actually harvest those yields and pay the bills." "Yes we can! Unequivocally yes we can, because we did! One family can purchase a property a hundred percent debt-financed, and we can convert [...] the farm in fifteen short years while paying our bills... collaborating with others..."

This is not to decry scale or to suggest that growth is always a problem. Other modes of life-living require systemic thinking. And the permaculture orientation to scaling-up is much more sensitive than most to the potentially deadening imprint it leaves behind in the stabilization of processes. Permaculture is in the main communitarian and resistant to monoculture. In this regard it is infinitely more interesting than what is currently underway in the monoculturing of our lives. But there remains a strong tendency to maintain the body-world separation that places the human outside nature to see what nature can do for us. It isn't cut and dry. These are thoughtful, knowledgeable and committed practitioners, whose work is making a difference. There is a continuous nod, in their rhetoric, to avoid building new structures, to the importance of working with what is already there, to recognizing emergent propositions in the chaotic process of change, to maintaining the long-view of seven generations. But still, there is a sense that the only way the work really makes a difference is if it is valued at scale, in the regime of the major, in modalities that are already recognizable. "You are working within an existing system," Livingston repeats, nodding her head to underscore the importance of being realistic in the face of things. "Show me another economy," Shepard responds, in collective recognition that what we have is what we have. Common sense. "Stand up and solve real problems." "For real."

In a pitch for the strengthening of economically viable networks for agricultural change, Sheperd even goes so far as to warn of the possibility of "find[ing] ourselves slaves in another penal colony," underscoring the imperative to "stick together... and start purchasing agricultural properties... [to form] a core nucleus... to produce enough to feed ourselves and create a surplus for sale and trade." A certain brand of survivalism stands out, as does its whiteness. Holmgren responds: we have to "do something real, get serious about the future... Be more focused on what is needed at a personal level, household level, community level." "Not count on these outside structures to take care of us," Sheperd responds.

In *As We Have Always Done* (2017), Leanne Betasamosake Simpson offers an adjacent path into similar principles, but with an important difference. The difference is that in Nishnaabeg pedagogy of land, the learning always moves out, beyond the learner, beyond the individual, into and onto the earth itself. There is no scale in this account of how nature natures, no delimitation of site, no reduction of nature to land. In the "radical imaginings out of domination," what is proposed in Simpson's account is not a rewilding of the land so much as an attuning to the life-ways the land as pedagogy always-already fosters (Simpson 2017, 10). It is a question of listening, of attuning to how stories that are mapped in a time out of measure facilitate encounters. "It is critical to avoid the assumption that this story takes place in precolonial times because Nishnaabeg conceptualizations of time and space present an ongoing intervention to linear thinking" (Simpson 2017, 152). "My main reason for postponing the end of the world is so we've always got time for one more story. If we can make time for that, then we'll be forever putting off the world's demise" (Krenak 2020, 36). "Stories direct, inspire, and affirm an ancient code of ethics" (Simpson 2017, 152).

Stories are without scale, their fabulations intercessors to the world's continuous reinvention. Minor gestures in their capacity to vary, stories are remade in the retelling. They are located in their encounter with the world as motors of its worlding. "Nanabush's trip stories the landscape with relational knowledges. When Nishnaabeg see a birch tree, we recognize a library of stories involving birch" (Simpson 2017, 184). The stories are not a simple folding of the past into the present, they are a regathering of "birchness" for the relationscapes of our times. "There is an organization of time and space that's different than the colonial world's – different planes of reality. The implicate order, if you want to use that term, is influencing and intertwined within our own continually created physical reality. [...] Our stories have always talked about the future and the past at the same time" (Simpson 2017, 201)

Scaling-up, despite its laudable desire to bring ecological principles to a wider diversity of environments, privileges the grand gesture, the straight timeline, and the modalities of value that are perceptible at that scale. In the evaluation of what counts as making a difference, the binary of the local and the global is upheld as is the colonial separation between body and world. This segregates the agricultural end of permaculture from the cultural side, foregrounding use value over all else. This despite permaculture practitioners carefully citing their indebtedness to Indigenous principles and continuously speaking of the necessity of living future-oriented on the Indigenous timeline of seven generations hence. The speculative reason is sidelined here, the emergent valuation of the transversality of the three ecologies backgrounded in favor of reason at its most normative edge. Where speculative reason attunes to the "hum" of existence, normative reason "prescribes method," "a godlike faculty which judges and understands" (Whitehead 1967, 222; 1958, 10). "There is Reason, asserting itself as above the world, and there is Reason as one of many factors within the world" (1958, 10).

Minor gestures bring a proliferation of variation into systems otherwise gridlocked. Speculative reason is the force of the conceptual flash that moves them into operation. Their immanent valuation is oriented by its feeling-forth of the art of living. It is the minor gestures that foster the nimble emergent valuations of an artful life, their incipient movement active in interstices of the hardened edges of staid modes of engagement. Punctual reorientators, they are fabulatory forces for the amplification of other modes of existence. Nature's naturing is replete with minor gestures.

When Simpson writes "[b]eing on the land is a highly intellectual practice that is a living interaction between heart, mind, and movement," I hear the transversal force of the three ecologies, the social, conceptual and environmental in interplay (Simpson 2017, 215). In the pulse of minor gestures animating the infrathin of the n-1 of their thirdness, a "generative refusal"[33] is at

33 "Building movements that reject the politics of recog-

work, a refusal to segregate, to evaluate, to stand outside looking in, distantist settler-pose at the ready. The production of subjectivity coursing across this thirdness cannot be mapped onto any preexisting capitalist formation (Simpson 2017, 242). Nature in its 3Ecological weave is undoubtedly also imbricated in all of the horrors of how life reduces itself – to capital, to whiteness, to settling – but it is not born of an impulse to reduce existence to the endurance of our low expectations. Simpson teaches us this: nature thinks, and its thinking pulsates in our acts. To sever that mode is to violently wrest existence from its exultant force.

The concept of scaling-up can only exist alongside and in a dependence on existent systems, and so whenever it comes up – however reluctantly – amongst the leaders of permaculture, what is echoed in its maneuverings is the world as-it-is. Reason as survey, as methodology, as colonialism, is hard to budge. There is no life in it.

Indigenous teachings take us down a different path. The generative refusal of its imbrication of land with life recognizes that "human beings

---

nition and center generative refusal inherently creates Indigenous bodies more connected to each other and the land, and that act out, through relationality, Indigenous thought" (Simpson 2017, 178).

require the most help from the rest of creation to live, and in that sense, we have the least amount of grounded, spiritual power and influence" (Simpson 2017, 243). The human is not centered.

There is an attempt to get here in permaculture circles, and it is called "permaculture zero." Understood as the principle before all principles, permaculture zero argues that we have been doing too much, and that our doing is causing more problems than solutions.[34] Brian Fey, practitioner of permaculture and originator of the term, explains: "I coined that Permaculture Principle Zero, 'Do Nothing,' a while back after reading about many permaculture 'solutions' which seemed like a waste of time, based on a lack of science, and poor accounting for energy use within the system."[35] "Saving energy" by "not doing a project" is the way permaculture zero is narrated, a "regression to the mean" often considered a better solution. "Doing nothing," imaged as Fey leaning back on his chair with his eyes closed, is conceptualized as "waiting" – "wait until [a path] appears... If you have nowhere to be, there is no reason to rush there. 'Stop and smell

34 https://www.quora.com/What-is-Permaculture-Principle-Zero.

35 https://www.quora.com/What-is-Permaculture-Principle-Zero.

the roses' is a common expression of the value of just stopping and enjoying a moment, an hour, a day, or longer if need be."[36]

Permaculture zero struggles with the same colonial tendency that maps human against nature. There is, in this approach, a recognition of the abundance that is already there, but the question of the human looms large. Not doing is still narrated in terms of human activity. Nature is still there to behold, in the ecological destruction it suffers at our hands.

Different practitioners will take this up differently, but the danger of the ethos will continue to make itself heard in the ongoing nature-culture divide it cannot but reinforce: for many, the "non-doing" will become a mantra for the "care of the self," a sure way to maintain a body-world separation. "Do not burn yourselves out... Save the other half of yourselves and your lives for pleasure and adventure," "please secure your own oxygen mask first before helping others," "this work of 'cranking out vegetables' ... often encouraged and reinforced attitudes in me that were less than sustainable."[37] "Not-doing" becomes

36 https://www.quora.com/What-is-Permaculture-Principle-Zero.

37 https://www.ic.org/permaculture-101-and-attending-to-zone-zero/.

a turning-in, a "return" to "our inner selves and our own bodies."[38] Inside-outside dichotomies are nothing else than the first method used to reinforce body-world separation. If what "Zone Zero" teaches us is to pay attention to self as the other to nature – "I paid more attention to the garden than to my own well-being [which] led me to knee problems that recently have prevented me from gardening at all" – it is ultimately only teaching us to remain colonial in our deeply engrained settler-tendencies.[39]

In a collective letter entitled "Whitewashed Hope,"[40] a group of Indigenous leaders speak

38 https://www.ic.org/permaculture-101-and-attending-to-zone-zero/.

39 There are deviations from to this human-centric approach to permaculture zero, but only, it seems, when Indigenous knowledge is centered. Sarah Queblatin works from Indigenous principles and with Indigenous populations in Kalinga and South Cotabato in her implementation of permaculture zero, which she understands as attuning to "tacit knowledge and practices that protect and restore their ecosystems, having lived in their places over time, and across generations. Inviting them to lead and design the solutions that impact our shared habitats [for a] more regenerative, and not just a sustainable, approach." Here, the non-doing seems to operate in a complicity with the land's teachings. See https://www.permaculture.co.uk/articles/decolonising-permaculture.

40 https://www.culturalsurvival.org/news/white-

to just this problem, that land regeneration in permacultural rhetoric continues to reinforce humanism in all of its colonial whiteness. “Where is nature?” they ask, referring to the tendency for nature to be posited “outside” bodily experience. “Nature is viewed as separate, outside, ideal, perfect. Human beings must practice ‘biomimicry’ (the mimicking of life) because we exist outside of the life of Nature.”[41]

Simpson writes of an “ecology of intimacy,” “kobade,” “a link in a chain... between nations, between states of being, between individuals” (2017, 8). Naturing nature: a “web of connections to each other, to the plant nations, the animal nations, the rivers and lakes, the cosmos, and our neighboring Indigenous nations” (2017, 8). This immanent field is without scale, without quantity. There are no “natural resources” that could be separated out from the imbricated ecology of all that lives artfully. Artful living, a “refusal of colonial recognition,” (Simpson 2017, 9) is experimented in the amplification of the speculative reason, that feeling-tone that radiates from the quality of the

washed-hope-message-10-indigenous-leaders-and-organizations.

41 https://www.culturalsurvival.org/news/white-washed-hope-message-10-indigenous-leaders-and-organizations.

living weave. There are no settlers here, and to be alongside is not to be an ally. Adjacency: "the reparative work of transforming proximity into accountability" (Campt 2021, 267).

•

1. A speculative garden is never discernible as a site. It sites a disturbance, a deviation, a reorientation that is too wide in its depth, too deep in its scope, to have a clear boundary.
2. A speculative garden colours existence. "Colours present themselves in continuous flux, constantly related to changing neighbours and changing relations" (Albers 1963, 5). Colour is contrast, lived relation.
3. A speculative garden is always and only transversal. The earth seeps into the study. Ground provisions: "[in] our reading together, we are returning not so much to a physical activity, but to a spooky state, to a material entanglement and entangled materialism, to a possession without property. This is our black metaphysics, our metaphysics of non-local travel in the Afro-Asian centuries. At Ground Provisions – in every visitation and refuge – when we read slow, when we read to each other, when we read

out loud, when we read together we conjure the life-giving arts" (Harney and Thompson 2018, 125)

4. A speculative garden refuses the survivalist attitude. Emergent valuation includes all those corners of life that feed our practices. We never grow things in the simple location of our settler imaginaries.
5. The feeling-tone of speculative gardens cannot be framed: they appear in the active selecting-out of what most intensely differs.
6. A speculative garden impersonalizes the land: relationscape (Manning 2009).

Concepts Are Nothing if They Are Not Lived:

The 3Ecologies Land Project

Interview by Stacey Moran and Adam Nocek with Brian Massumi and Erin Manning

Stacey & Adam: We're longtime admirers of your individual and collective work, and we're confident that many of our readers are too. What's inspiring to us is how the theoretical intersections of your research – evident in your deep and sustained engagement with Whitehead, James, Guattari, Deleuze, and Simondon, among others – are born out of what seem to be quite different creative and intellectual backgrounds. Can you speak to some of these differences, how they create mutually reinforcing contrasts and ultimately help sustain long-term intellectual investments?

Brian: I'll come at this a bit sideways, from the angle of where our approaches intersect. We come together, across the differences in our backgrounds, in a shared way of activating philosophy. When we approach a set of philosophers, we delve into the possible convergences that work through them. This doesn't mean that we treat an author's work as incomplete and needing supplementation by another. We don't look for holes to fill in. We don't critique weaknesses and compare strengths. The work that attracts us is complete and self-standing, and we honor that. We are attracted to work in which concepts relay each other to form a web of consistency whose total texture confers upon each concept the particular power it has to make a difference for a movement of thought. We treat each work as a dynamic system. It's an essentially open system, in spite of – or, paradoxically, because of – its completeness. The completeness is more a saturation than a closure. What saturates it is the charge of implication couched in the conceptual web, by virtue of the tightness of its weave.

Whitehead provocatively stated the conditions for an adequate philosophical system in the opening pages of *Process and Reality*, where he says that each component concept cannot be understood without reference to the others – but that they connect by what is unsaid in each. One concept's implications are brought out through a relay to others. In turn, the relay modulates the collective texture and reacts back on all its component concepts, creating new vectors of implication. This makes the system inexhaustible. The implications, once set in motion in this way, are of infinite complexity. The work becomes a machine for generating new distinctions while remaining self-consistent, true to itself. This is the characteristic of what we think of as "generative" texts, and it is to these that we return time and time again to find new riches, preferring this eternal return to broad reading and "keeping up with the field." We're intensive re-readers, limited by the infiniteness of our generative texts.

We apply what Whitehead said about a philosophical system's dynamic self-relation to the relation between generative works. Certain authors' works share orientations that place them in operative proximity to each other. These are less doctrinal principles than motivating presuppositions that set the conditions of possibility for what the thinking can produce, and work it continuously from within. The concepts of different authors working from a similar presuppositional field have the same characteristic Whitehead sought: they connect on the level of what each leaves effectively unsaid for another, by dint of mutual oversaturation. So rather than critiquing, we draw out threads and weave them into a movement of thought emergent in the between. If this is successful, it creates a transindividual field of consistency that becomes our habitat of thought. This way of approaching works constitutes a "minor" treatment of the texts: sidestepping general discussion of "major" concepts (periods, schools, doctrines, stock philosophical problems).

If we had to state, in a way that is communicable from the major perspective, what presuppositional orientations the authors that are generative for us share, we would say that they take process as the starting point. This involves construing the basic unit of reality to be the event and seeing events in terms of qualitative change, or emergence. This makes everything a question of potential and its playing out to give rise to determinate forms. These are understood as self-organizing takings-form – which makes process itself the agent. This recontextualizes the question of the subject, focusing on preindividual goings-on and asubjective intensities, of which the subject in the usual sense is a product or precipitate. We could go on – the implications multiply – but this short sketch is sufficient to signpost a direction. When a thinking operates from this presuppositional field, it is in the realm of what James called "radical empiricism," Deleuze called "transcendental empiricism," and what we like to call "speculative pragmatism." But we multiply the terms to keep things productively off-balance and avoid falling into doctrine or school-building. So we'll also call it "activist philosophy," "process thinking," "minor thought," or "research-creation." Each term carries different implications, inviting readers to draw out their own threads of consistency in response to our work. There is nothing we want less than followers.

Erin: For us, it's the livingness of the philosophy that stands out. We seek thinkers whose concepts activate existence and make living possible. What modes of thought are capable of sustaining that quality of "saturation" Brian mentions?

Nietzsche's work is where I always return to find the spark of living – "Was that life? Well then once more!" From Nietzsche, a world reveals itself that moves, that dances. This world, which refuses to limit itself to a preexisting subject, is full of questions, its aphorisms a persistent refusal to hold thought down by tethering it to the explicit. Whitehead's philosophy is different, and yet it carries a similar openness to thought, a persistent commitment to the activity of living. This modality – what Deleuze might call *a* life, what I have called "life-living" – is the force of life beyond the individual subject, beyond the human.

Philosophy lived is philosophy practiced. As Brian says, there is no appetite here for critique. We don't read to find the inconsistencies in thought and to fill the gaps with something from outside a given philosopher's operative logic. Certainly, there can be times when it's necessary to prolong a concept by other philosophical means, but mostly our work is to become more acquainted with what textures this singular thought and to try it out.

Brian: As our answers imply, we don't hold each other down to our own respective backgrounds. What philosophy does in concepts, art does in paint, movement, sound, light. The principle is the same: an artwork carries the same intricacy of oversaturation among its component elements that a philosophical text does among its concepts, and the same goes for the relation between artworks that belong to the same series (by which I mean, emerge from allied problematics and intervene in correlative fields). This processual analogy between art and philosophy enables transfers and mutual supplementations to occur between them, in an expanded field. This makes art philosophical, in its own way, and philosophy creative. This is the supplementarity that we both work through. What is unique about Erin's contributions is that she writes philosophy and also does artwork, in a number of media: dance, textile, painting, installation, to name the most salient. I write philosophy and interfere in Erin's art. At least that's how I think Erin experiences it when she is deep in an artistic practice, and I come peer over her shoulder and kibitz. Although, we have done some truly collaborative artwork, like the "Twisted Nietzsche" performance, and we inhabit the between of art and philosophy together, in close processual embrace.

Adam: I recall the first time I heard about the SenseLab. I was a PhD student at the time, attempting to bridge media philosophy, biology, and design and growing frustrated, not only because I was no longer legible to the "humanities" and certainly not to philosophy (which is where I started off), but because integrating practice into this research agenda was pretty much inconceivable from where I stood. I still remember enthusiastically showing a professor of mine the SenseLab and *Inflexions* websites and thinking of it as a model of research-practice at the busy intersection of philosophy, art, science, design, and activism. I also remember the professor telling me to steer clear of that kind research because it's a one-way ticket to unemployment. I clearly didn't pay much attention to this advice, since I subsequently approached you to coedit an issue of *Inflexions*, but I imagine this story is not completely unique. Or at least, the SenseLab has been an important home for graduate research that's not always legible to what the MLA or CAA deem acceptable humanistic and arts research. I wonder if you could speak to the SenseLab's role in providing a shelter for graduate students, their research, and cultivating alternative research agendas?

Erin: I remember being delighted by that email, Adam! And what a gorgeous issue it is. When we started *Inflexions*, it was precisely with this concern in mind. We felt there needed to be more opportunities for the kind of interdisciplinary, art-oriented, and intensively philosophical (un-peer-reviewable) work we have published there over the years. At the time there were really no other examples of research-creation on the web, and so our main influence was the French journal *Multitudes*, particularly for its early commitment to the overlap of the political and the philosophical and its interest in what they called "the minor" – which is the title of a section of the journal dedicated to work that was transversal to the core concerns of any given journal issue. While we published much student work over the issues, the aim was never to situate *Inflexions* as a site for any particular kind of artistic or scholarly work. Our aim was simply to publish the most exciting work, and especially work we knew might otherwise fall through the cracks.

What you say about career suicide has been repeated as a "friendly" warning to everyone we've ever worked with! And while it may be true as regards a standard academic path, it's certainly not the case that people with whom we have worked have not thrived in charting new ways, both inside and beyond the academy. My sense is that it has very little to do with SenseLab or with *Inflexions*. It's more the other way around. SenseLab never did any kind of publicity, nor did *Inflexions*. We waited until people found us. We did that because we knew that we needed to learn from those who made their way to us – that in their arrival, they would bring something important, a quality of experience they would then leave behind. You are an example of that. You came already poised to be at odds with academia as it likes to define itself. SenseLab was a step on that journey. Your gift to SenseLab was believing that there are other ways, and forging that path so that others could also find their way there and beyond.

I have never thought of SenseLab as a site. It's more a proposition – a lure for feeling, as Whitehead would say. Perhaps it is what gives some of us the confidence we need to make the jump into other ways of living and learning. But "it" is nothing by itself.

Brian: For me, the lure was to take seriously Deleuze's dictum that "concepts are nothing if they are not lived," and to act accordingly at a collective level. This phrase sums up what Erin and I mean by "speculative pragmatism." It means both that concept-making is a practice, and that the practice of concept-making has a rendezvous with other practices, to which it transmits actionable potential and receives formative influences in return, in a symbiotic back and forth. This is the "movement of thought" that Erin writes about extensively.

The problem SenseLab was responding to is that the last thing at stake in academics, as it is dominantly practiced, is thought. It's about knowledge: data, information, description, and plausible interpretation, with the form of the results enframed by a methodology or analytic approach set in place in advance, preformating the trajectory to conform to a certain image of what constitutes useful knowledge. I never worked that way on principle because I was always more interested in how thought can approach the limit of the knowable, and cross it into the creation of new trajectories, unforeseen. I felt myself marginalized in my department because of this. I also watched my students being channeled into that more traditional image of thought by the way the program of studies was structured. Along the route – usually during the thesis proposal writing process and its official departmental acceptance – they would very often deflate. They would lose their traction because they were often forced to relinquish the original impulse animating their work in order to fit the frame. It saddened me to see them lose the sense of urgency or necessity that had inspirited their project. What SenseLab offered my graduate students was the same thing it offered me: a milieu where thinking-together was attended to as an emergent practice whose results are not preplayed and whose use-value is not predefined, fundamentally reposing the question of what constitutes knowledge. It offered the excitement of intellectual and creative exploration – what the university purports to be about, but wouldn't know if it saw it.

Stacey & Adam: Your work at the SenseLab has always struck us as an inspiring mix of philosophical abstraction and embodied social practice, so much so that the one seems unthinkable without the other. We say this not simply because you've managed to combine philosophy – largely in the spirit of speculative pragmatism – with a style of arts-based research that's been fashionably dubbed "research-creation" in Canada (and now elsewhere), but because of what seems to be a much more sustained commitment to building conceptual practices inextricably tied to how you lead your lives – a kind of "life praxis." In this respect, the SenseLab always seemed to us less like a formal academic center or laboratory – even if it published and produced an incredible amount of research – and much more like a mobile site for actualizing the unseen potentials of a life; for experimenting with nomadic living, with neurodiversity, with antiracist pedagogy both inside and outside formal institutional settings, and for valuing what is rarely legible to metric-obsessed universities and celebrity academic culture. It seems to us that the 3Ecologies Project (3E) continues to build on much of this work. But we're curious how 3E continues to expand what it means to activate potentials for living.

Erin: For us, radical empiricism – or speculative pragmatism – is lived across all of life's interstices. This means we just don't separate concepts from living. Philosophy is a web that complicates and sustains all that moves through it and beyond it. Our practices often take us away from the books. Those practices germinate the questions that allow us to return to philosophy differently each time. We need philosophy to excavate the ineffable, not-as-yet-known, that moves through the practices, particularly at the junctures where there are impasses.

More recently – since Brian and I purchased a large tract of land off-grid and have been moved to explore the ongoing work of our 3Ecologies Project (*3ecologies.org*) through the land – we have been pulled into a new angle of practice. In the past, as you say, our collective practice was usually oriented by the laboratory that SenseLab became, which involved coming together with others to explore the activation of a concept through a variety of modes (aesthetic, movement-based, spatializing, etc.) or developing a movement of thought by engaging with materials. Many key concepts were born that way – enabling constraints, relational platforms, anarchiving, immediation, event. And what is perhaps most interesting is that these concepts, born in the making, became robust practices that could be carried elsewhere and experimented with under other conditions. A concept was never "purely" philosophical. It was philosophically orienting for those whose practice was attuned to writing, and it was aesthetically emboldening for those whose tendencies were more artistic. This doubleness allowed us to move with the concept to better understand what else it could do: Could it generate other concepts? Could it activate or sustain a practice? Could it spur new modes of existence?

Over the years, one of the most compelling directions this research-practice took was neurodiversity: we became increasingly sensitive to the normative constraints of the thresholds for experience we commonly entered into. Starting with the event and moving to the classroom, our collective work was committed to developing an emergent attunement to what lurks in the interstices of the normative modes of engagement. What is willfully backgrounded in order to foster neurotypical modalities of thought and movement? But as always, we arrived here not through conversation but through activity: we practiced other ways of coming into relation, developing new modes of collaboration. One of these modes, developed over several years, was called "composing." It grew out of a recognition that to enter into a space is to make the space, and that this making of the space should be careful not to presuppose typical orientations. Space became the question: What is expected in a room where learning happens? In a bedroom? In a kitchen? Classrooms were rebuilt to foster worming, caves for hiding on the edges, tents sitting in the middle. Chairs were put on the ceiling, reminding us of what is expected by the postures they mandate. Tables were set on their backs. And then, in the years that followed: an active composting. Use the same elements and create again. It's not the materials themselves, it's how they come into relation to activate a movement, to create a body. From here: new concepts of the neurodiverse bodying. And then, an intensification of the question of how neurotypicality and whiteness co-compose.

By creating conditions for experimentation, concepts are created that shift our sense of where sites for collaboration best do their work. This is slow and careful work. It is often hard to discern whether anything is happening at all. Some days are spent repeating a gesture, lost in the image of what that gesture could have done under other circumstances. But shifts are discerned: the commitment to what concepts can do in conditions that are sensitive to how worlds are made is strengthened. This alters individual practices. And it often affects how we see ourselves in the frames we are given to reflect ourselves.

Since we bought the land, the difference we've noticed is that for now, the practice is often less directly connected to concepts we recognize or can easily discern. Practice has become a mode closer to survival in a context where we are almost always in over our heads. The context is complex: we have purchased land three hours north of Montreal where the winters are long and cold (and beautiful!), and we are trying to sustain three off-grid houses, two of which are powered by solar (and one of which has no power). Propane, like everywhere in the north, is the backup, and one we prefer to use as sparingly as possible because of its carbon emissions as a fossil fuel. To these ends, we find ourselves consumed by two things: wood and sun. The wood is not only to keep us warm – harvesting it is also necessary to clear sight lines for the sun and recomplexify a forest ecology coming out of an extractive history of occasional timber exploitation. So we cut and clear and stack and lug, replant and protect (in a losing battle with the beavers, who provide us with a lively set of ponds and toad havens). And then we hope for sun. In winter, daylight only lasts eight hours, and if we get four hours of sunshine, we consider ourselves blessed. In the midst of this, we try to understand why someone would build a generator for the north that doesn't start when it's colder than -5 °C in a region where -30 °C is not uncommon! And so we play the electricity game: Can we spare fifty watts for a heating lamp for the generator, or will the generator now go on because of those fifty watts?

The practice of keeping the houses awake moves us into act but is not necessarily of the species we might tend to understand as aesthetic or political or even remotely philosophical. Other emerging practices more so: preparing a permaculture-type gardening area, planting fruit trees, making maple syrup, caring for the old-growth maple forest, regenerating streams and previously logged forest. What all of these practices have in common, I think, is that they are pragmatic in a more emphatic way than those we engaged with through SenseLab: they pull us into act with an urgency that is theirs. Moving at the rhythm of an environment we are still in the process of connecting to is quite different from staging the conditions for a laboratory and experimenting with the concepts it generates.

We have found this disconcerting. Often our books feel quite distant, and we wonder how to "get back" to our work. This is the wrong approach (surely someone who wrote *For a Pragmatics of the Useless* should know that!), but it still lingers. This is our new challenge. Certainly, we will have more opportunities to move through concepts the way we have in the past; but for now, we are interested in the new rhythms of the environmental ecology and what those rhythms teach us about what it means to do the work we do.

While this is still very new, it has led us to become more curious about the relay between activity and thought. What practices take us further afield? On the spectrum of the speculative and the pragmatic, where is the philosophical, as a practice in its own right, most operative? My sense is that when we are fully engaged on the most pragmatic end of the spectrum – worrying about generators, say – the philosophical is much less directly present. What is perhaps interesting is to ask how its present-absence is nonetheless having an effect. A process-philosophical approach would be curious about that, I think. It would ask how that pragmatic event carries a "perspective of the universe," and what that perspective does.

Whitehead's concept of perspective is never reducible to what inhabits a preexisting subject. What he calls a "perspective of the universe" is lived in each occasion of experience, tangentially. This means that a particular take of the world on itself agitates in its every activity, pulling us in and moving us along with it. The presupposition is that because of this there is always a speculative edge in experience, always a share that exceeds the given. Exploring this generative tension of the speculative and the pragmatic is how we live philosophy and how philosophy lives us.

Brian: Put another way, what's important isn't the apparent contradiction between what we tend to think of as "merely" pragmatic and the creatively speculative. Feedback and feedforward effects can take the most mundanely utilitarian considerations up in a speculative movement. It is composing across the registers, each prodding and interrogating and potentializing the other, that draws the hyphen in speculative-pragmatic. It forms a hybrid assemblage. Or in more precise Guattarian terms, a transversality. Even battling generators can be generative! The trick is to find creative factors where they are least expected.

Stacey & Adam: Given the critical nature of your research-practice, it's remarkable to us that you've been able to sustain your work within the neoliberalizing institutional spaces of the university for almost two decades now (since at least 2004). Of course, we're all aware that to say the university is "neoliberal" is such a twenty-first century cliché that it's barely worth mentioning. It just rehearses what everybody knows and says little about the actual policies and practices governing the university and the real lives affected by them. Yet, with the formation of 3E, you raise some incredibly important questions about what the institutional practices of the university can and cannot tolerate, and more specifically, about what it values. Can you speak to how specifically 3E creates spaces for entertaining values that challenge the practices, policies, and strategies of governance within the university? And by doing so, what do you (as an institution and/or subjects within a system) risk?

Brian: There are three challenges to the neoliberal university that a project like 3E poses that come immediately to mind. They have to do with the use-value of knowledge that we already mentioned, collectivity, and evaluation. One of the main impetuses behind SenseLab from the beginning was to challenge not only the instrumentalization of knowledge along preset parameters but its commercialization. We were responding to this specifically in the context of art and creative practice.

In the early 2000s, there was a push within Canadian universities to annex artistic and creative practices to the culture industries. The official interest in what was introduced to artists as "research-creation" was motivated by a hope that it could serve as an innovation laboratory for potential products, especially in relation to digital media. The neoliberal vocabulary of "deliverables" began to be applied to art. Alliances between the arts and computer engineering were prioritized, creating an uneasy arrangement where the culture of the "hard" sciences was juxtaposed with that of creative practice, without that juxtaposition being productively problematized. In the face of this, SenseLab proposed a "pragmatics of the useless." The revaluation of value at the heart of the proposition was a call for experimental practice to follow its own momentum and create its own techniques, in the cracks between the disciplines. It's not about "interdisciplinary" practice as it usually plays out, where experts work according to their existing methods, each in their own corner, and then come together to share results – a basically communicational model of agglomeration. What it implied instead was a truly collective coming-together.

By "collective," we mean entering together into a third space unpreformated by disciplinary strictures. Into that space a set of enabling constraints is injected to pressurize the encounter toward an eventful issue, one that would come of the singularity of that encounter. The collectivity is a synergy: a more-than the sum of the parts, so integrally, processually entangled that what can be credited to one participant as opposed to another becomes unassignable. This raises the issue of evaluation. How do you credit or grade a more-than of individual efforts? How do you grade the contribution of nonhuman participants? In an experimental or improvisational process, things entering in sideways or environmentally, not to mention chance impingements, can be as powerful a productive factor as the conscious, agential actions of the human ingredients of the event.

The only evaluation is a valuation: an experience of the process as having had value, as having been "worth it," not in comparison to extrinsic standards, but of its very occurrence as having intensified or activated or engrossed in a way that imparts creative momentum to the next encounter in the line and divergently toward the future individual or collaborative endeavors of the participants. This is what I have called "surplus-value of life" – the yield to be had by living concepts under the sway of movements of thought that sweep you up, rather than you directing them.

3E inherited this orientation. It takes what SenseLab was doing and places it at one remove from the university. Not as a frontal move against the institution, but sidling it, in potential concertation with certain of its functions, but unsubmitted to its neoliberal mandates, operating by a logic of its own. In a way, this is a return to SenseLab's origins, because during its first few years it was not based at the university. It entered the university midstream, in a Faustian bargain that created many potentials for SenseLab but also brought much pain. The big difference, as Erin explained, is that the remit of 3E has expanded to include the third of Guattari's "three ecologies": the environmental. SenseLab addressed social ecology in its prototyping of techniques of relation and experimentation with collectivity. It addressed the conceptual/psychic ecology in its dedication to the movement of thought and, especially in the later years, its attention to and fostering of neurodiversity. Now 3E addresses the environment by adding a vector of land-based practices. The forest, meadows, gardens, and streams of the 3E land have their own ideas about what an enabling constraint is, and how synergies grow. It isn't just an addition of another area or object of concern. It's an interrogation by the land of SenseLab's treatment of the other two ecologies. It can be very disruptive, but in a challenging way replete with the production of "surplus-value of life," in which the bees and the beavers, the berries and weeds, are ultimately collaborators.

Erin: As mentioned earlier, this third ecology can seem to be more pragmatic than speculative, its urgent call a refutation of the slow work of reading and writing or making art. It moves us into act before we can lay out the conditions for acting, before we can set up thresholds for qualities of existence. In this sense, it feels quite different from all we've practiced so far. Whereas in the past our work was the setting up of conditions, on the land the conditions are often beyond us, pulling us into them in ways that can feel completely out of control.

The work of 3E will be to learn more about how the conditions were actually never completely ours to control, and to become more sensitive to the emergent field of conditions as they occur. To feel out of control, after all, is only a sign that you are not *on* a territory – that the territory envelops you and moves through you. As we learn how to move apace with it, in its necessity and to its rhythm, we become sensitive to the environment in ways we might not have been in the past, and we become more capable of discerning the panoply of practices the environmental ecology calls forth. This new laboratory is terrifying insofar as the contours are indiscernible. It's impossible to know its limits in advance.

To practice in a territory without limit is to give into practice itself, as process. It is to learn in the midst, and to be in the learning of the middle. This sounds easy in theory, but in practice it is often very confronting. It doesn't necessarily feel creative at first approach to work at the pace of an ecology that in all senses of the word exceeds us. But this teaching, this learning, is the radical pedagogy 3E is interested in.

So many of us dream of finding other ways – beyond the institutions that seek to frame and contain our work. But it seems to me that despite ourselves, we too often embody those frames. We carry them with us. We are so trained to recognize our value in those frames that we can't quite reconcile ourselves to other modes of living.

I often think of abolition when I am stuck in one of those frames. To truly practice an abolitionist politics is to commit to other forms of justice and, by extension, to other forms of value. It is to practice living otherwise. Abolition's radical pedagogy requires of us that we allow that practice to lead us. This will often feel like taking a step away from learning, because learning has become so synonymous with a format, and with finalized form. In that format, we know we've learned because we have an output to show for it. We know we have been just because we have called something out, clearly delineating the boundary between what is right and what is wrong. The environmental ecology, in its transversal relation to the social and the conceptual, challenges this mode of thought. It asks us to follow the necessity of an orientation and to be reorganized by it. From there, it asks us to set ourselves aside so that we can better feel the contours of what has thresholded itself into activity. This activity is self-sustaining. It doesn't need us. Indeed – we are often a danger to it. To participate in it, to collaborate with it, is to learn another movement, another way of engaging.

Stacey & Adam: Rarely do we encounter scholar-practitioners who are willing to challenge the forms of social capital the academy is capable of bestowing on them. Sure, we see para-academic spaces and platforms popping up everywhere now, new autonomous summer and winter schools, certificate programs, and the like flooding the internet (we count ourselves among those who are guilty of just about all these para-academic models). What's striking, although not in any way surprising, is that many of these schools and programs, especially in the theoretical humanities, repeat the same old transactional logic of the university in a slightly altered form: there are academic experts and students who pay fees, and then credit is given in some form, etc. In fact, it's our experience that some of the worst tendencies of celebrity academic culture are reproduced in these informal settings, since "big names" (often propped up through Twitter debates, etc.) draw students, fees, and social-media chatter, all of which help reproduce the social capital required to create the celebrity needed to attract students. In any case, this brings us to 3E. It strikes us that you're attempting to create a very different model of pedagogical practice, a way of collectively organizing the spaces of education, research, and living that don't fall prey to this logic. Can you tell us how specifically (e.g., the techniques and tactics used) you've been able to evade certain transactional models of education, and what still requires work?

Brian: First, as Erin mentioned, we have never advertised or promoted. We did send out calls for the first two SenseLab events, but they were worded in a way that made it clear that this was not the kind of event you would know how to put in your CV. The calls were intentionally worded to make it difficult to know what the format would be and what exactly would happen. What was communicated was that, although the context would be carefully prepared, it would be prepared in such a way that nothing would happen if the participants didn't make it happen collectively. This disables the transactional assumptions people have been trained to enter with: treating the event as the delivery of a service, positioning the participants as consumers.

We have tried to follow through with this participatory, self-organizing ethos in everything we do – including administration. There is no executive or programming committee. We never have decision-making meetings. Everyone is empowered to throw out a proposition for an activity, start it moving, and see if it takes. Organizationally, we've experimented with affinity groups and with what we call SOPs (self-organizing propositions). These are like irrigation canals for the group's fluid energies that are hosted on our Slack and were conceived to be part of a new collaborative digital platform – the Process Seed Bank. The SOPs are ways of tending to emergent propositions and shepherding through stages of realization, without any particular individual or delegated group making a decision about them – purely according to their own lure, their own power to gather energies themselves. In the transition to 3E, we even applied this to decisions about finances and the allocation of funds. (There are a number of working papers on the 3E website that go into these techniques.)

Emergent decision-making of this kind is exhilarating when it works. And a bog of quicksand when it doesn't. You have to be willing to accept the risk of failure. Failure in this context is usually due to the collective process flagging, when attention is in short supply and energies low, so that someone has to step in and act in a more top-down manner to avoid a car crash. This understandably leads to resentment, both on the part of the person who had to step in and thus is forced to betray their own anarchist desires and principles and others in the collective who feel that a central power has swooped down on the self-organizing. The focus is then diverted from the motive force of the propositions and the project, and the situation becomes personalized.

Personalization is the enemy of processualization. It activates all manner of all-too-human pettiness, competition, and moralistic holding to account. A breakdown is likely to ensue. This happened periodically with SenseLab, almost on schedule every four years or so (that seems to be the life expectancy of a flow of self-organizing energies, at least for us). Recovering from the breakdown and contagion of personalization requires a cut and reset – what we call a "schizz" – that detours things back in emergent directions. This requires precise technique. But there is no general technique for it. It has to find an angle on the situation that tweaks or leverages it into a phase shift. Not easy, and not always painless. It's always a work in progress.

We recently went through a period like that with 3E, because as Erin has been explaining, the land brings with it a different order of pressures than we've had before. There are things that just have to be done at a certain time and in a certain way, or the solar won't work and the batteries will get spoiled, or the pipes will freeze, or plants won't grow, or the sap won't turn to maple syrup, or vehicles will get stuck in the snow and ice. The milieu itself dictates. It requires of us a certain quality of attention and a capacity to creatively blur the boundaries or find a new accommodation between work and play, the creative and the mundane. In addition, the move from the university to what we call "parainstitutional" status, with one foot in and one foot out, required the formation of an official nonprofit and, in anticipation of a functioning alter-economy – a huge, uncertain project! – a new, more traditional stream of financing (we settled on Patreon). These come with certain legal norms and expected practices. We consider it a part of our creative practice to invent modes of "creative duplicity" that enable us to straddle those realms without letting their logic take us over. For example, we have defined the role of the administrative board that nonprofits are required by law to have as a caring-for and guardianship over the self-organizing process, rather than the usual function of top-down oversight and executive decision in the last instance. There are always ways of meeting normative requirements while subverting them – a kind of pragmatic queering of the organizational.

We have an appetite for a culture of sharing experiences and techniques around organizational issues. Collectivity, outside the normative frames we all know too well, is a challenging practice, and that needs to be taken seriously. That's part of what 3E would like to help foster. We offer our techniques – for what they're worth – and would love to hear about others'.

In terms of pedagogy, I often think of Deleuze's phrase for philosophy: "a pedagogy of concepts." It means that concepts teach us what a concept can do as we go about constructing them. It's not about teaching already-arrived-at concepts to others. It's about swimming with the creative flow of concepts' emergence, being fed and led by it, and inflecting it in return. Likewise, research-creation processes teach us what a body can do as we go about doing it. The key is to avoid a transmission model of knowledge, and the hierarchy between those in the know and those to be brought up to standard that comes along with it. In an emergent model of thinking-living, everyone is a co-factor in knowledge formation. This doesn't mean there are no differentials of expertise or power, only that things are so contrived that those inequalities don't define the overall situation. They are acknowledged, even benefited from strategically at times, but they do not rule. They are backgrounded by the knowledge and powers of the emergent collectivity, and defused when they start to impinge on it. This always requires situation-specific techniques.

For 3E, we are working to build that backgrounding into the suggested structures of events that the project will host. Instead of a class structure, we thought of three formats for participatory workshops that can be initiated by any individual or grouping. We called them "knots," "junctures," and "vectors." It's probably too much to go into here – the definitions can be found on the 3E and 3E Patreon sites (https://www.patreon.com/3EInstitute). They are actually less formats than different qualities of movement of thought to be collectively staged.

Erin: When the practice leads, the teaching is much harder to discern. But perhaps that is a settler-statement. I have a sense that Indigenous teaching understands this implicitly, and we are as attuned as we can be to those practices. But given our distance from those teachings, we learn this less from process philosophy than from Indigenous philosophy more directly. What teaching means in this context is hard to frame. But we have all the years of tending to the threshold, so rather than worrying too much, we keep focused on the ways the different thresholds teach us about the conditions for existence they make possible. What this looks like in practice is impossible to say, since it has to emerge over time. Anything we can say today about SenseLab comes not from a direction SenseLab sought to take but from what emerged, of its own, over years of moving quite slowly through operative problems.

The operative problem of 3E is the question of property. What might it mean to take seriously the challenge of Fred Moten and Stefano Harney's concept of the undercommons in the context of a land purchase? Having worked for years on alter-economies (toward the 3E Process Seed Bank), we know how difficult it is to shift the contours of the financial. We are so wedded to the systems we hate!

Our aim with the property is to "give the land back to itself." Once the debt is paid or an alter-economy grows around it that is capable of sustaining it, we will transfer it to a land trust or entrust it to a foundation to permanently take it out of the real estate market and the extractive economy, and preserve it in perpetuity as a commons where the land is cared for and made available for learning and practicing sustainable gardening and forestry techniques (not to mention growing philosophy!). This may include others, who cannot afford to purchase property, building and living on the land for free, provided it is with a minimal ecological footprint and it contributes to the collective potentials of the project. This is not a back-to-the-land model. What we hope to experiment with are ways of living-thinking that are committed to the transversality of the three ecologies. The land is one node in a larger matrix that includes the relation to the city.

For the moment this will look like fostering alter-economies that allow the 3E land to host, in the existing buildings, people who are interested in learning from that pesky pragmatic ecology that keeps us on our toes. Over time, it may involve experimenting with off-grid architectures suited to this kind of climate, such as Earthships or self-sufficient tiny houses. By necessity, this will involve learning about landscape architecture – how to keep old-growth forests flourishing, how to build without clearing unnecessarily, and how to regenerate the streams and wetland areas, not just for the "useful" species of sport fish but for the frogs and salamanders and sedges and other often overlooked inhabitants of the land. Next summer, our first large-scale garden will be seeded: a forest fruit, nut, flower, and vegetable garden. We will learn what might be feasible as a perennial vegetable in this climate. Asparagus is our focus for the first year, but we will also try other vegetables that might be sustained (perennially) through microclimates. We think a lot about flowers and insects and toads and beavers. What might an affective-permaculture look like? A useless garden?

Transaction is hard to get around completely. You're always implicated in a transactional economy of some kind, at some point of contact with the dominant culture. On the land, we engage in all kinds of transactions on a daily basis. We can't do everything ourselves – we just don't have the expertise. And so we pay people to do all kinds of things: cut trees that have fallen on the sap line, build woodsheds and generator sheds, fix generators and repair solar systems. At the moment we are the students. But the transactions can't be confined to a simple model of exchange. The folks who come out here to assist us do much more than what we pay them for: they care about the land, and the project. We find that more often than not, they do more than what they were contracted for. The transactional exchange economy overspills into a gift economy. At this generative interstice, another kind of learning happens. We learn to value the modes of existence a variety of skills facilitate, and to see the world from the perspective of what that skill calls forth. An example would be the skill of the lumberjack. Rémi, who has cut many trees on our property, does more than receive an hourly rate in exchange for the lumbering of the trees. He is designing the forest as he cuts, sensitive to what needs more sun and what will soon have to be taken down because it is crowding out a healthier tree or because it will soon die. We don't have to tell Rémi about 3E – he is already there, working at the transversality of the social, the environmental, and the conceptual. His work gifts us not only an expanse of land that allows the solar panels to be more optimal, but a vision of how time moves through the forest.

Over the last many years of thinking about what else a radical pedagogy can be, a lot of thought has gone into the concept of accreditation. We are told, without fail, that we need accreditation, and yet we all know that accreditation is what we buy, not learning as such. Learning, it turns out, is what happens despite ourselves. There is an argument that accreditation is necessary for those kept out of the systems of learning. And that may be true. But surely we have to question the capitalist nature of what we consider the credit of learning? What is learning outside the accounting of it, and what can this outside do?

Stacey & Adam: What's intriguing about 3E is that it's not entirely outside of the university system. While the institute is formally autonomous (financially and culturally, it seems), it still draws on its connections to the SenseLab and Concordia. In this way, 3E seems to inhabit, if that's even the right word here, the conceptual and spatial logic of an institutional "borderlands," a domain of practice and inquiry that's neither fully outside nor inside the university. Can you speak to the bordering practices of 3E, and more specifically, to what relations with the university still seem viable, which ones can be severed without destroying the ecological balance, and whether you see any more general lessons to be learned about institutional bordering?

Erin: We have thought a lot about the power of the parainstitutional. The university does one thing really well: it attracts creative people. The problem is that the creativity generated in that environment too often occurs in spite of it. It's a systemic issue, not an individual one. There are many fantastic people who teach and study and administer, and for the most part, I have found my interactions with those people to be generative. More often than not, I am moved by the care professors express toward students, and I am convinced that there is a commitment, by so many of us, to create environments for learning. The problem is that the institution itself is not nimble. Institutions never are. They are slow-moving machines that watch the bottom line. This means that whatever change they steward will always rely on an already existing set of criteria. These criteria are deeply mired in existing models of (capitalist) value. Evaluation – the matrix by which the university meters itself – is by extension also a capitalist equation. We don't study so much as evaluate ourselves according to a system that reduces us to the count.

What we need is the opposite! We need sites of conviviality and participation whose emphasis is on discovering value, not reducing ourselves to a depleted vision of knowledge mobilization. The parainstitutional has the advantage of moving at a more flexible pace. That doesn't mean the parainstitutional is unthreatened by the orientations institutions take. We are so habituated to the forms of organization that organize us that we tend to reproduce them... But it seems to me that the advantage of the parainstitutional is that it can fail more easily – that it can rebuild, or if necessary, self-destruct in ways the university never seems to be able to.

Something baffles me about the university: its capacity to make us thankful about the work we so often hate to do. It's amazing how often a conversation amongst professors turns to our collective anguish about the normative structures imposed on us, about the terrible conditions of teaching, about the unfair division of labor, about the debt our students take on. And yet we don't quit. I have thought about this for years and have come to the conclusion that we don't quit because we have been trained to respond affectively to the scarcity market of academia. To have a job that is tenured is to have "made it" into a small club you can never leave. Very few professions work this way. What is it that keeps us in these institutions? I think it's the belief that we are "called" to do this work, that the work matters. But what is it about it that matters? Aren't most of us doing the work that matters anyway? Aren't we already engaged parainstitutionally, finding zigzags that allow us to actually do the work we love, between the meetings and the marking and the administering?

A good reason to stay is that it pays the bills. Another good reason to stay is that it can foster certain sites of emergent sociality, on the sidelines. But really, what I long for is something altogether different. I long for the courage to follow what matters where it needs to go, under its own conditions.

So much of this thinking comes of my frustration around neurodiversity and Indigeneity and race and how they play out in the institution. There is willingness, certainly, to address these, but this willingness remains tethered to that bottom line, both capitalist and colonialist. We are "welcoming" difference into the institution, but always on the institution's own terms. How many times have I been told to "be realistic" or "to accept" that "this is the best the institution can do under the circumstances"?

3E doesn't seek to be an "other" to the institution. The "para" of its proposition is as much about texture, qualities of relation, as it is about institutional form. I have no desire to fight the university at this stage. I am happy to go and teach and be moved by what I learn with students. What I want is to multiply environments for learning so that I can learn what else learning can be. In that context, I don't want to "welcome" difference. I want to be welcomed by it, to be in the midst of it. An ecology is precisely that: a complexity. Here, settling is not an option. It's not about owning or evaluating. It's about being in conduit of an environment's self-expression. The work of 3E will be to explore what that can involve. By necessity, I see this as an opportunity to delve into forms of encountering the world that are vastly at odds with a university environment. We will not know in advance what we are learning. There will be no matrix of evaluation to let us know that we are reaching milestones. We will not "mobilize" knowledge.

Brian: Erin's point about not wanting to be an other of the institution, an alter-institution, is crucial for me. My dictionary glosses "para-" as "from the Greek *para*, 'beside'; in combinations often meaning 'amiss, irregular' and denoting alteration or modification." Beside, amiss, alteration. That sums it up. 3E stands beside the university, in the sense of taking a step away from it, but also being in step with it in certain ways, hoping to supplement the opportunities for thought and practice its faculty and students may have access to, through a productive come-and-go. But it also troubles the institution, as a thorn in its side, standing as a constant reminder that something is amiss with the university's hardening of the arteries of knowledge and eager subservience to the neoliberal economy. It signposts the possibility of alteration – of the very form of the institution. It's not about an other of the university that would be an institution in the same sense it is. It's about opening the concept of the institution to process in a way that avoids fixed hierarchies and the clinging to normative frames and bureaucratic proceduralization that weigh down the traditional institution's self-professed concern with "excellence" with a gravitation toward the lowest common denominator, all in the name of "efficiency" and ensuring (minimal) "standards." A "parainstitution," in the sense we mean it, experiments in organizational form, endeavoring to find a dynamic form of acting-together that is equal, in the plastic potential of its own organization, to the emergent movements of thought it wishes to host. It eschews the content/form dichotomy of the university institution, where knowledge is packaged by the curriculum and supporting administrative structure like the contents of a box. "Para" opens out onto an expansive field. "How" things are done is as much a part of the study as the content of the propositions pursued. This is as political as it is pedagogical. It allies 3E with a long tradition of experimentation in participatory forms on the extraparliamentary left, particularly with respect to the anarchist and autonomist movements and throughout the history of the feminist movement. That is as much the milieu we move with as the university is. Our "para" straddles both.

Stacey & Adam: Many of our readers come from design and creative fields. They also tend to be dissatisfied with the reigning models of higher education and are passionate about forging new pedagogies within alternative institutional settings. It strikes us that the "speculative institutional design" you're invested in is likely to generate a wealth of techniques that have been honed, experimented with, and transformed according to the specifics of a domain. Given your experience with establishing the SenseLab (and *Inflexions*) and now 3E, do you see yourselves engaged in a kind of critical and speculative institutional design? This isn't meant to reduce the complexity of your work to something that sounds bureaucratic. On the contrary: we're wondering how the many techniques for institution formation you've developed might be coordinated through shared values (e.g., the design of alternative education/research spaces) and whether they overlap with techniques cultivated in other design, artistic, and education fields, including social and speculative design, architecture, and urban design, as well as with the traditions of radical and antiracist pedagogy, performance art, activism, and other areas. Given this, we wonder if there could be a radical pedagogy of institutional design, where institutions are shaped to inhabit the borderlands? Or is this antithetical to the project itself?

Erin: Our Process Seed Bank project is very much aligned to the questions you ask above. For years we have longed for an environment where techniques are shared. So many people are doing fascinating and important work, and yet we tend to be too busy to really engage with each other's practices... We dream of ways of aggregating that experimentation, which I suppose is the ethos of what you are doing here!

I think from our end, what we have learned, and what we continue to learn, is how to create conditions for the emergence of new techniques. The techniques themselves, we have noticed, are very local, very singular, and specific. They are really not interchangeable into another context. We came to this realization the hard way, over many attempts to bring our techniques into other settings (like the conference or the exhibition). It never worked. The techniques must emerge organically from the event that spawns them.

What is somewhat more transferable is an ethos, a care for the event's capacity to be hospitable to new conditions. I think over years of practice what we have learned is to honor the durational yield of practice, to recognize that an emergent attunement to the conditions at hand is necessary. I suppose we have learned to be more agile? And certainly we have practiced not putting ourselves at the center of the work. This is the hardest task, to practice the impersonal.

The impersonal, as we've explored it over the years, has a lot of overlap with Gilbert Simondon's concept of the transindividual, that force of emergent collectivity that transduces any notion of individuality. This being of relation, as Édouard Glissant might say, is the force of collectivity as we understand it. To attune to this quality of experience, and to practice it, is to be engaged in what I have called "minor sociality." This quality of sociality – which I feel is allied to what Laura Harris calls "the aesthetic sociality of blackness" – is neurodiverse through and through in the sense that it refuses a strict boundary between body and world, individual and other.

To practice impersonality is to be engaged in the environmentality of the event, to be moved by the conditions of its coming-to-existence, to be brought to life through it. If we begin here, what reveals itself is the field of relation. This is where study does its work most emphatically, I find. So if we can foster conditions that allow this shift to occur, techniques will be created that become a conduit for the field's opening up into other realms.

This is a roundabout way of saying that the techniques are there to be invented, but for that to happen, conditions have to be created. We will learn from past movements and be enriched by them, but in order to truly come into contact with their potential, we cannot stand outside looking in. We have to allow ourselves to be made by the environments we desire, and for that, we have to succumb to the risk of being unmade by them as well.

Brian: I'll just add a chorus: conditions have to be

created. Supple, adaptable techniques have to be set in place to terraform a terrain of participation and orient it in certain propositional directions whose outcome is not preplayed. What it takes to condition a milieu of relation is very different from the techniques that will then ply that milieu to produce a movement of thought and precipitate knowledge formation. This difference has to be kept in mind. It is what we try to get at with the term "techniques of relation." Relation isn't just coming together. It's more than conviviality. It's coming together under propitious conditions for the production of a surplus-value of collectivity – that "more than the sum of the parts" by which the individuals involved outdo themselves.

This is part of what we mean by the impersonal: the exceeding of our personal potentials by relational synergies. We don't want to express our sorry selves. Because there is nothing so impoverished as a separate self. "We are sick of ourselves," Nietzsche bemoaned. What we want to express is beyond ourselves. We want to express ourselves into ways of moving, thinking, and knowing that we ourselves, from our limited personal standpoint, can have only a vague inkling of before we actually experience them together. Erin and I are just embarking on a joint book project that we're calling *Living Beyond Biography*. Many people won't be willing to embrace this kind of impersonalism in the name of emergent intensities of existence, especially in this age of identity and what I like to call the "piety of the personal." But even for those who do not find this to their appetite, the suggestion that there are techniques of relation specifically addressing the conditioning of events of research and creation may still resonate.

Stacey & Adam: Where do you see 3E in five years?

Brian: I would be extremely satisfied if, over the next five years, 3E were able to effectively merge the philosophical investigations that SenseLab carried out through reading groups, punctual events, and publishing projects with ongoing land-based activities that are regenerative in all senses of the word. A key part of this for me is activating a transductive relation between the city and the countryside, in the sense that there is continuous variation of techniques that pass between the rural and urban milieus and processually couple them, so that they become phase-shifts of each other's take on the three ecologies – the social, the conceptual, the environmental – rather than polar opposites and adversaries. At SenseLab, we had an event called "Generating the Impossible" (2012) that actually took place deep in the northern forest not far from what is now the 3E land, then experimented with transferring the processes initiated in the woods to the wilds of the city. It was one of our most successful events, in my experience. One of the concepts we tried to operationalize was "exaptation," which is a transductive concept that comes out of anti-neo-Darwinian evolutionary theory. It refers to the repurposing and change in nature of an adaptation when it moves from one milieu to another. I would love to return to those experimentations. Perhaps most of all, I would like to take the very hard work and thinking we've done over the last five years on alter-economies and exadapt it to the new context created by the addition of the land component to our activities.

Erin: In five years I anticipate I will be close to shifting from the university to full-time stewardship of the 3E land project. By then, we will have had the opportunity to learn from the passage of collaborators – folks we know and haven't met yet who are moved to experiment with the transversality of the three ecologies on this northern landscape. We will have gone further into our experimentation with sustainable power, perhaps having harnessed an additional source of nonextractive potential from the land, such as hydro or wind, enabling us to phase out our propane use. And our gardens will have grown and died away a few times, teaching us what thrives in this climate. In five years, perhaps we will be lucky to taste our first apple or pear or cherry or plum from our fledgling orchard, and we will have stomped down on the overgrown raspberries enough to have established some paths that allow us to cultivate that bountiful berry, whose aim it is to take over all the sunny land! The maple forest will have established itself a bit more, and we will have learned to better distinguish between the trees and to spot the chaga that the locals find so easily. We will also have tapped a few birch trees and have tasted the sap. Whether or not we will have built a greenhouse is hard to say. I dream of a kind of northern Earthship-greenhouse-studio, but I also wonder whether it is necessary. I suppose it will grow itself if the necessity presents itself. For the moment the necessity is more oriented toward encountering what is already here.

In five years, perhaps there will be a new structure. Sometimes we imagine a yurt or two, shared by folks in the wider network. Shared, noninheritable, but infinitely transferable housing. By then, if we are lucky, when we are renting out the houses to help financially support the project (which we do when there are no residencies or events), we may be attracting mostly folks for whom the project matters and who are interested in participating in it, if only economically. And I suspect we will have gotten better at making maple syrup. But nothing will ever surpass that first year's madness and the sixteen affectionately named batches: Gone Fishing, Ça Mousse, Come On Baby, Eternal Return, It's a Moose, Push It, Ça Traîne, One More Degree, Haut Débit, Double Whammy, Danger Zone, Second Chance, Disaster, Endtroduction, Eternal Object, Abstract Surface.

Brian: The names say it all!

Ifeoma Anyaeji. Ana Ramos. Manu Gosselin. Andrew Murphie. Andre Arias. Anna Munster. Anouk Hoogendoorn. Branca Cabral. Khadija Baker. Cadu Mello. Miguel Razafindrakoto. Dana Dugan. Dave Levine. Emma Flavian. Alan Prohm. Halbe Kuipers. Bodil Marie Stavning Thomsen. Mayra Morales. Doerte Weig. Matisse ApSimon Megens. Lucy Wheeler. Erik Bordeleau. Ben Muñoz. Pia Ednie-Brown. Shaya Ishaq. Jonas Fritsch. Kelann Currie-Williams. Javed (Bob) Sheikh. Celine Pereira. Mariana Marcassa. Lone Bertelsen. Mattie Sempert. Jondi Keane. Estee Klar. Charlotte Farrell. Adam Wolfond. John Lee Clark. Matthew Robin-Nye. Joel Auerbach. Francisco Trento. Tessa Laird. Csenge Kolosvari. Toni Pape. Sher Doruff. Diego Gil. Joel Mason. Michael MacDonald. Garrett Johnson. Leslie Plumb. Tom Lamarre. Indira Shanahan. Mario Therrien. Christoph Brunner. Amélie Brisson-Darveau. Phoebe Osborne. Sheena Bernett. Gisèle Trudel. Andrew Goodman. Susan Turcott. Julietta Singh. Stéphane Claude. Nathan Snaza. Roberto Correa. Chris Wilbert. Tamir Eting. Milena Kartowski. Jon Beller. Sandy Miller. Eric Therrien. Erik Félix. Luke Shirock. Rick Massumi. Rémi Roy. Dany Bigras.

Works Cited

Adeyemi, Kemi. 2019. "Beyond 90°: The Angularities of Black/Queer/Women/Lean." *Women and Performance* 29, no. 1: 9-24.

Akomolafe, Bayo. 2021a. "Let's Meet at the Crossroads." *Bayo Akomolafe* (online), May 29. https://www.bayoakomolafe.net/post/lets-meet-at-the-crossroads.

Akomolafe, Bayo. 2021b. "Meditations on Blackness." *Shelburn & Primrose United Churches* (online), April 15. https://www.shelburneprimrose.com/resources/meditation-on-blackness-by-bayo-akomolafe.

Albers, Josef. 1963. *Interaction of Color*. New Haven: Yale University Press.

Albright, Ann Cooper. 2017. "The Perverse Satisfaction of Gravity." In *The Aging Body in Dance: A Cross-Cultural Perspective*, edited by Nanako Najajima and Gabriele Brandsetter, 63-73. London and New York: Routledge.

Arakawa, Shusaku, and Madeline Gins. 2002. *Architectural Body*. Tuscaloosa: The University of Alabama Press.

Bergson, Henri. 1911. *Creative Evolution*. New York: Henry Holt and Company.

Bergson, Henri. 1922. *Durée et Simultanéité*. Paris : Presses Universitaires de France.

Bradley, Rizvana, and Denise Ferreira da Silva. 2021. "Four Theses on Aesthetics." *e-flux Journal* 120 (September). https://www.e-flux.com/journal/120/416146/four-theses-on-aesthetics/

Cache, Bernard. 1995. *Earth Moves: The Furnishing of Territories*. Cambridge: The MIT Press.

Campt, Tina. 2019. "Black Visuality and the Practice of Refusal." *Women and Performance* 29, no. 1: 79–87.

Campt, Tina. 2021. *A Black Gaze: Artists Changing How We See*. Cambridge: The MIT Press.

Cézanne, Paul. 1978. *Conversations avec Cézanne.* Paris : Macula.

Clark, John Lee. 2017. "Distantism." *Wordgathering: A Journal of Disability Poetry and Literature* 11, no. 3 (September).

Combes, Muriel. 2020. "On Nature." *Log* 49 (Summer): 147-164.

Currie-Williams, Kelann. 2022. "Afterimages and the Synaesthesia of Photography." Unpublished.

Deleuze, Gilles. 1989. *Cinema 2: The Time-Image*. Minneapolis: The University of Minnesota Press.

Deleuze, Gilles. 1991. *Bergsonism*. New York: Zone Books.

Deleuze, Gilles. 2005. *Pure Immanence: Essays on a Life*. New York: Zone Books.

Deleuze, Gilles, and Félix Guattari. 1987. *A Thousand Plateaus*. Minneapolis: The University of Minnesota Press.

Ferreira da Silva, Denise. 2014, "Toward a Black Poethics: The Quest(ion) of Blackness Toward the End of the World." *The Black Scholar* 44, no. 2: 81-97.

Ferreira da Silva, Denise. 2016. "On Difference Without Separability." In *Incerteza Viva (Living Uncertainty)*, Sao Paolo Fundacao Biennal de Sao Paolo.

Glissant, Édouard. 1997. *Poetics of Relation*. Ann Arbor: The University of Michigan Press.

Glissant, Édouard. 2010. *L'imaginaire des langues—entretien avec Lise Gauvin*. Paris : Gallimard.

Guattari, Félix. 2000. *The Three Ecologies*. London: The Athlone Press.

Harney, Stefano, and Fred Moten. 2013. *The Undercommons: Fugitive Planning and Black Study*. Minor Compositions.

Harney, Stefano, and Fred Moten. 2021. *All Incomplete*. Minor Compositions.

Harney, Stefano, and Tonika Sealy Thompson. 2018. "Ground Provisions." *Afterall: A Journal of Art, Context, and Enquiry*: 120-125.

Hartman, Saidiya. 1997. *Scenes of Subjection: Terror, Slavery, and Self-Making in Nineteenth Century America.* Oxford: Oxford University Press.

James, William. 1890. *The Principles of Psychology.* New York: Henry Holt and Company.

Krenak, Ailton. 2020. *Ideas to Postpone the End of the World.* Toronto: House of Anansi Press.

Manning, Erin. 2009. *Relationscapes: Movement, Art, Philosophy.* Cambridge: The MIT Press.

Manning, Erin. 2013. *Always More than One: Individuation's Dance.* Durham: Duke University Press.

Manning, Erin. 2016. *The Minor Gesture.* Durham: Duke University Press.

Manning, Erin. 2020. *For a Pragmatics of the Useless.* Durham: Duke University Press.

Manning, Erin, and Brian Massumi. 2021. "Infrafacing." In *Affects, Interface, Event*, edited by Bodil Marie Stavning Thomsen, Jette Kofoed, and Jonas Fritsch, 307-326. Lancaster and Vancouver: Imbricate!.

Manning, Erin, Anna Munster, and Bodil Marie Stavning Thomsen, eds. 2019. *Immediation*. London: Open Humanities Press.

Massumi, Brian. 2011. *Semblance and Event: Activist Philosophy and the Occurent Arts.* Cambridge: The MIT Press.

Massumi, Brian. 2014. *What Animals Teach Us About Politics*. Durham: Duke University Press.

Massumi, Brian. 2015. *Ontopowers: War, Powers, and the State of Perception.* Durham: Duke University Press.

Massumi, Brian. 2019. *Architectures of the Unforeseen: Essays in the Occurent Arts*. Minneapolis: The University of Minnesota Press.

Massumi, Brian. 2021. *Parables for the Virtual: Movement, Affect, Sensation, Twentieth Anniversary Edition*. Durham: Duke University Press.

Mollison, Bill. 1988. *Permaculture: A Designer's Manual*. Sisters Creek: Tagari Publications.

Moten, Fred. 2003. *In the Break: The Aesthetics of the Black Radical Tradition*. Minneapolis: The University of Minnesota Press.

Nyong'o, Tavia. 2018. *Afro-Fabulations: The Queer Drama of Black Life*. Durham: Duke University Press.

Orange, Tommy. 2018. *There, There*. Toronto: McLelland and Stewart.

Proulx, Annie. 2016. *Barkskins*. New York: Charles Scribner's Sons.

Rolnik, Suely. 2017. "The Spheres of Insurrection: Suggestions for Combating the Pimping of Life." *e-flux Journal* 86 (November). https://www.e-flux.com/journal/86/163107/the-spheres-of-insurrection-suggestions-for-combating-the-pimping-of-life/.

Sharpe, Christina. 2016. *In the Wake: On Blackness and Being*. Durham: Duke University Press.

Simondon, Gilbert. 1995. *L'individu et sa genèse physico-biologique.* Grenoble : Éditions Jérôme Millon.

Simpson, Leanne Betasamosake. 2017. *As We Have Always Done: Indigenous Freedom Through Radical Resistance.* Minneapolis: The University of Minnesota Press.

Viveiros de Castro, Eduardo. 1998. "Cosmological Deixis and Ameridian Perspectivism." *The Journal of the Royal Anthropological Institute* 4, no. 3 (September): 469-488.

Viveiros de Castro, Eduardo. 2015. *The Relative Native: Essays on Indigenous Conceptual Worlds.* Chicago: Hau Books.

Whitehead, Alfred North. 1941. "Immortality." In *The Philosophy of Alfred North Whitehead*, edited by Paul Arthur Schilpp, 682-700. Evanston and Chicago: Northwestern University Press.

Whitehead, Alfred North. 1958. *The Function of Reason*. Boston: Beacon Press.

Whitehead, Alfred North. 1967. *Adventure of Ideas*. New York: Free Press.

Whitehead, Alfred North. 1968. *Modes of Thought*. New York: Free Press.

Whitehead, Alfred North. 1978. *Process and Reality: An Essay in Cosmology*. New York: Free Press.

Index

Erin Manning studies in the interstices of philosophy, aesthetics and politics, concerned, always, about alter-pedagogical and alter-economic practices. Recent monographs include *The Minor Gesture* (2016) and *For a Pragmatics of the Useless* (2020). 3e is the direction her current artistic research takes – an exploration of the transversality of the three ecologies, the social, the environmental and the conceptual. An iteration of 3e is a land-based project north of Montreal where living and learning is experimented. Legacies of SenseLab infuse the project, particularly the question of how collectivity is crafted in a more-than human encounter with worlds in the making.

CPSIA information can be obtained
at www.ICGtesting.com
Printed in the USA
BVHW070712131122
651493BV00001B/5

9 781570 274053